UNDERWAY

AVIATION PROGRAMMES FOR the US Marine Corps and US Navy are making solid progress in their respective fielding plans. Block III F/A-18 Super Hornets are now assigned to the Naval Air Warfighting Development Center based at Naval Air Station Fallon, as is the Next Generation Jammer pod already flying on an EA-18G Growler from the Nevada superbase, and preparations are underway for the first pods to be assigned to a fleet squadron at Naval Air Station Whidbey Island, Washington.

The fleet of F-35 Lightning II stealth fighters continues to grow with both the US Marine Corps and the US Navy. The Marine Corps now has two F-35 training squadrons and nine front line squadrons in operation, and the US Navy plans to deploy its second F-35C squadron in the autumn/fall timeframe, with a third squadron due to stand-up soon.

The US Marine Corps continues to implement and refine its Expeditionary Advanced Base Operations concept for deploying forces to austere locations, and the US Navy continues with its Distributed Maritime Operations doctrine. Both concepts involve deploying forces in well-established units, primarily the Marine Air-to-Ground Task Force (MAGTF) and the Carrier Air Wing (CVW).

The US Navy and Marine Corps Air Power Yearbook 2023 covers the work-up cycle undertaken by a MAGTF and a CVW, we take a deep dive into the US Marine Corps and US Navy weapons schools, worldwide EA-18G Growler operations, and Training Wing 6 based at the cradle of naval aviation, Naval Air Station Pensacola, Florida.

Mark Ayton, Editor

Mark Ayton

CONTENTS

US Navy/Lieutenant Antonio Moré

US Marine Corps/LCpl Ricardo Ramirez

US Navy/Mass Communication Specialist 2nd Class Armando Gonzales

ISBN: 978 1 80282 814 6

Editor: Mark Ayton

Senior editor, specials: Roger Mortimer
Email: roger.mortimer
keypublishing.com
Cover design: Steve Donovan
Design: SJmagic DESIGN SERVICES,
India

Advertising Sales Manager:
Brodie Baxter
Email: brodie.baxter@
keypublishing.com
Tel: 01780 755131

Advertising Production:
Becky Antoniades
Email: rebecca.antoniades@
keypublishing.com

SUBSCRIPTION/MAIL ORDER
Key Publishing Ltd, PO Box 300,
Stamford, Lincs, PE9 1NA
Tel: 01780 480404
Subscriptions email:
subs@keypublishing.com
Mail Order email:
orders@keypublishing.com
Website:
www.keypublishing.com/shop

PUBLISHING
Group CEO and Publisher: Adrian Cox
Published by
Key Publishing Ltd, PO Box 100,
Stamford, Lincs, PE9 1XQ
Tel: 01780 755131
Website: www.keypublishing.com

PRINTING
Precision Colour Printing Ltd, Haldane,
Halesfield 1, Telford,
Shropshire. TF7 4QQ

DISTRIBUTION
Seymour Distribution Ltd, 2 Poultry
Avenue, London, EC1A 9PU

Enquiries Line: 02074 294000.

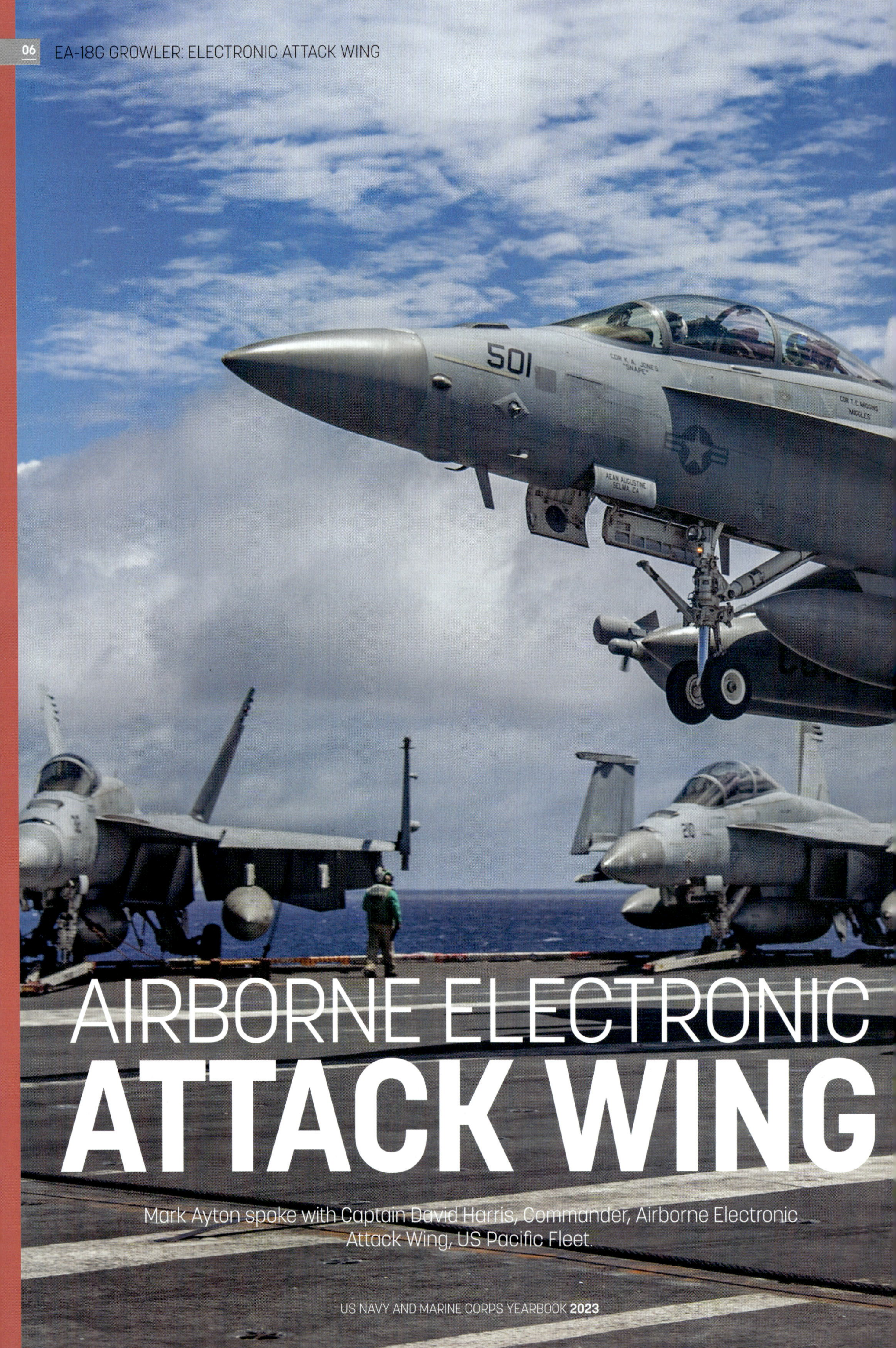

AIRBORNE ELECTRONIC
ATTACK WING

Mark Ayton spoke with Captain David Harris, Commander, Airborne Electronic
Attack Wing, US Pacific Fleet.

Above: **An EA-18G Growler assigned to Electronic Attack Squadron 139 (VAQ-139) 'Cougars' makes an arrested landing aboard the aircraft carrier USS *Nimitz* (CVN 68).** US Navy/Mass Communication Specialist Justin McTaggart

IN HIS JOB as Commander of the Electronic Attack Wing, US Pacific Fleet, Captain David Harris is responsible for ensuring the 15 Growler squadrons assigned are properly manned, trained and equipped.

Five are expeditionary squadrons, those that deploy to land bases primarily to support coalition or joint forces. Captain Harris has operational command for all expeditionary squadrons and 10 boat squadrons assigned to Carrier Air Wings for both the Atlantic and Pacific Fleets. When embarked on an aircraft carrier, each boat squadron is commanded and tasked by the Carrier Air Wing Commander.

Captain Harris noted an interesting point: "Each time an east coast squadron goes out to the aircraft carrier, it has to transit across the country to embark the carrier underway in the Atlantic which requires the squadron to depart Whidbey early. That adds extra days away, which may not be significant in the short term, but over an aggregate period, it adds up to more weeks away from home for the Atlantic Fleet squadrons."

Captain Harris is the immediate boss of the five expeditionary squadrons, the Fleet Replacement Squadron, VAQ-129, and the Airborne Electronic Attack Weapons School.

Manning for each squadron is the responsibility of the airborne electronic attack wing, not only on the aircrew side, but also on the enlisted side.

Left: **Captain David Harris, Commander, Airborne Electronic Attack Wing, US Pacific Fleet.** US Navy

Below: **Captain Christopher Bahner, left, then Commander, Electronic Attack Wing-Pacific, poses with pilots in front of an EA-18G Growler assigned to Electronic Attack Squadron 144 (VAQ-144) following their first flight at Naval Air Station Whidbey Island, Washington on October 4, 2021.** US Navy/Mass Communication Specialist 2nd Class Aranza Valdez

Explaining, Captain Harris said: "We make sure each squadron has the maintainers, administrators, logisticians, intel, cooks, the CSS, the master at arms for security, everything that the squadron needs to deploy and ultimately deter conflict and if required, fight. Each squadron has approximately 200 enlisted sailors and is supposed to be an organic unit with everything that's needed to deploy on an aircraft carrier or to a forward deployed location like Misawa, Japan, Al Udeid, Qatar, or Spangdahlem, Germany.

"Each squadron deploys with intelligence specialists and crypto analysts to organically analyse the electronic warfare information gathered by the aircraft, and the logistics support necessary to move parts and people back and forth. Each squadron also has a damage control section to make sure all the necessary chemical-biological gear is present. God forbid if there was any sort of attack on South Korea, we would have everything that we need present on the squadron."

Demand and the Operational Tempo

Discussing the Growler force and its operational tempo, Captain Harris said: "The Growler is a low density, high demand asset, and the world's only tactical offensive airborne electronic attack asset, which is primarily why we

Above: An EA-18G Growler assigned to Electronic Attack Squadron 144 (VAQ-144) lands on the flight deck of the aircraft carrier USS *George Washington* (CVN 73) while underway in the Atlantic Ocean on June 26, 2023. US Navy/Mass Communication Specialist Seaman August Clawson

have the expeditionary squadrons. In addition to providing each carrier air wing with a Growler squadron, generally we have one expeditionary squadron deployed to Misawa Japan and hold a second squadron at a state of readiness to deploy in response to a real-world event. The world and potential enemies get a vote in our operations. Examples are Incirlik, Turkey to counter ISIS and Spangdahlem, Germany to support the NATO high readiness task force following Russia's invasion of Ukraine.

"We have a just under 160 Growler aircraft assigned to the wing. Each squadron has a complement of five aircraft which varies depending on situations around the world, except for VAQ-141 based at Iwakuni, Japan which always has seven aircraft.

"We have constant software upgrades and aircraft continuously going through capability upgrades, the main one being the Growler Capability Modification run by Boeing [and] underway here at Whidbey. We've modified over 30 aircraft to date.

It's a complex process trying to handle all of them throughout the fleet, so we have a dedicated maintenance professional on the staff who figure out exactly where an aircraft can be transferred. So, for example, has the aircraft been modified to GCM standard, have other upgrades been completed on the aircraft?

"Within the Growler fleet, we have sub-fleets of aircraft in different configurations which requires careful management, squadrons must not go backwards in capability. Once a squadron

Right: An EA-18G Growler assigned to Electronic Attack Squadron 135 (VAQ-135) 'Ravens' and an OP-3C Aries II assigned to Maritime Surveillance Squadron 81 (VQ-81) of the Japan Maritime Self-Defense Force during a bi-lateral exercise. US Navy/VAQ-135

gets a new capability, it stays with that configuration, but that limits flexibility in terms of moving aircraft between squadrons, and from a maintainer and aircrew perspective. Effort is focused on introducing the Next Generation Jammer and the H16 and H18 software suites that run the pod, which is a huge challenge."

Growlers continuously operate with F-35 Lightning II squadrons from the US Navy, US Marine Corps, US Air Force, and allied nations. Why? Because the F-35 has unique suppression of enemy air defence capabilities that complement those of the EA-18G Growler.

Explaining, Captain Harris said: "The F-35 can't do what a Growler does. The Growler performs offensive airborne electronic attack, and that's where its strength lies. The Growler's ALQ-218 receiver system is really what sets it apart. No other aircraft has a receiver system integrated throughout the aircraft. The F-35 is equipped with some unique systems used for the electronic attack role, and because it's a low observable aircraft, it can operate a little closer to the fight, than a Growler can.

"We constantly train together because the tactics, techniques and procedures used by each type are complementary. The Growler can't do what the F-35 can do, and vice versa, but there's a lot of synergy that comes from operating together. The Airborne Electronic Attack Weapons School called HAVOC deploys to Nellis Air Force Base for over a month, twice a year to develop tactics, techniques, and procedures with the US Air Force Weapons School's F-35 division.

Stood up in 2011, the Airborne Electronic Attack Weapons School trains Growler pilots and electronic warfare officers to become Growler Tactics Instructors during a 12-week course. The syllabus comprises academics, simulators, and missions. HAVOC runs four courses each year.

"The aircraft's role varies dependent on the mission, generally split between kinetic and no-kinetic roles, the latter in the modern digital battlefield.

"Demand for the Growler continues to increase, remember it's the only offensive electronic attack asset in the joint inventory that can affect the electromagnetic spectrum. The Growler is

the only type that can do that, so we get tasked to do joint exercises like Northern Edge, which increases our workload. We also support the US Marine Corps Weapons and Tactics Instructor course at Yuma, and work with its F-35 division to develop new tactics, techniques, and procedures. One thing is for sure, the squadrons are very busy so we can't afford to do a whole lot of extra taskings.

"The final third of the Growler Tactics Instructor course is spent at Nellis Air Force Base participating in the weapons integration (WSINT) phase of the US Air Force Weapons School course, just one example of joint operations, in this case, fully integrated with all the US Air Force aircraft types involved in WSINT."

Aircraft Maintenance and Inspections

The Airborne Electronic Attack Wing is currently managing a maintenance reset programme to the Growler fleet at Whidbey. As of August, the reset was over halfway through.

The wing's maintenance officer sequences each aircraft based on

Below: **An EA-18G Growler assigned to Electronic Attack Squadron 140 (VAQ-140) 'Patriots' launches from the flight deck of the USS *George H.W. Bush* (CVN 77).** US Navy/Mass Communication Specialist Nicholas Avis

Above: **An EA-18G Growler assigned to Electronic Attack Squadron 139 (VAQ-139) 'Cougars' launches from the flight deck of the aircraft carrier USS *Nimitz* (CVN 68).** US Navy/Mass Communication Specialist 2nd Class Joseph Calabrese

availability and in coordination with its scheduled preventative maintenance inspection. As each aircraft goes through its long-term preventative maintenance inspection [PMI] its maintenance reset is also performed, 65 aircraft have been completed to date.

As part of the maintenance reset, components like seals are replaced to reduce future corrosion. The programme, running since 2021, is managed and co-ordinated by a dedicated senior chief petty officer assigned to the wing.

Work to complete the maintenance reset for one Growler aircraft takes 90 days.

Depot level maintenance is undertaken by the FRC Northwest at Whidbey, and many of the big repairs are completed at Whidbey by personnel from FRC Southwest based in San Diego when required.

Depot level maintenance of ALQ-99 jamming pods, mission monitor equipment and electronic warfare systems is completed at Naval Surface Warfare Center Crane in Indiana.

Effective maintenance pays dividends. In recent years the aircraft availability rate and the number of aircraft available for flight operations has improved. "By and large, we meet the number of mission capable aircraft required, and we have aircraft that can be quickly surged if required," said Harris.

GROWLER OPS
AROUND THE WORLD

Mark Ayton spoke with Commander Jim Dobbs, executive officer of VAQ-129 and the former director of operations for the Airborne Electronic Attack Wing based at Whidbey Island.

I N HIS JOB as the director of operations for the Electronic Attack Wing, Commander Jim Dobbs had an all-encompassing responsibility for the operational commitments of the EA-18G Growler expeditionary force and for maintaining and equipping the carrier-based squadrons.

Commander Dobbs cited the Next Generation Jammer and the Growler Capability Modification as the two most significant programmes currently underway in the Growler community.

Following its return from deployment aboard the USS *Nimitz* (CVN 68) on August 9, 2022, Electronic Attack Squadron 133 (VAQ-133) 'Wizards' entered its maintenance phase and started preparing for the Next Generation Jammer. The Wizards have been operating the Next Generation Jammer since early 2023 and deployed to Eielson Air Force Base, Alaska for Exercise Northern Edge 23-1 during May.

Describing the pod, Commander Dobbs said: "It's a huge game changer in terms of power, technique and the physical electronic capability of the aircraft to influence the electromagnetic spectrum. It's leaps and bounds from the current ALQ-99 jammer and represents the future of electronic attack.

"To date the NGJ has undergone developmental testing with Air Test and Evaluation Squadron 23 (VX-23), then operational testing with VX-9, two pods are currently in operation with HAVOC, the Growler weapons school at Fallon, and two are assigned to VAQ-133 which starts NGJ training at the end of 2023. VAQ-133 will fully equip with the NGJ for the entirety of its workup and deployment.

"The enabler for the NGJ is the Growler Capability Mod or GCM, a five-year programme, which is being undertaken by Boeing at Whidbey Island."

Naval Air System Command's PMA-265 described the GCM as, "the first major effort to upgrade the capabilities of the EA-18G Growler in the type's history."

"Commander Chris Gierhart, PMA-265 Growler Systems Integration lead officer said: "The GCM will allow the Growler to maintain the advantage in the electromagnetic spectrum and lay the basis for future upgrades to keep the aircraft relevant into 2040.

"The GCM comprises multiple modifications to several of the aircraft's systems to support the integration of advanced fibre optics for communications, a new tactical datalink using Tactical Targeting Network Technology (TTNT) waveform technology, which takes a little bit of the load off Link-16 and is very specific to the Growler mission set, and the ALQ-249(V)1 Next Generation Jammer Mid-Band (NGJ-MB) pod.

"GCM will make the ALQ-218 sensor system more sensitive, it comprises a radar warning receiver, electronic warfare support measures, and sensors used to gather electronic intelligence, and enable the NGJ to specifically focus on new generation threats, specifically phased array radars and complex emitters.

"The Boeing team allocates a six-month period to complete a GCM, and to date, has not exceeded the six-month target timeline.

"Individual aircraft are sequenced into the GCM programme based on the number airframe hours and the aircraft's planned maintenance schedule.

"We look at a squadron's deployment date and the number of aircraft required for that deployment and identify which aircraft can go the entirety of the deployment without needing a major overhaul at around 600 hours, or overhauls of individual components. There are also airframe flight requirements. Let's say you have a major component that will hit its service life within the timeframe of the deployment.

"When an aircraft exits the GCM, in theory, the aircraft is reset and ready to go back to the fleet, able to make the entirety of the work-up and the deployment cycles. We factor in longer deployments and extra time to allow for surge

Below: **Sailors assigned to Electronic Attack Squadron 131 (VAQ-131) 'Lancers' perform pre-flight procedures on EA-18G Growlers during Exercise Vigilant Storm 23 at Osan Air Base, Republic of Korea, on November 1, 2022.** US Air Force/SSgt Dwane Young

Right: **Vigilant Storm is an annual, pre-planned training exercise that provides the ability to improve readiness and train to better operate as a joint force.** US Air Force/SSgt Dwane Young

Below: **An EA-18G Growler assigned to Electronic Attack Squadron 131 (VAQ-131) 'Lancers' takes off from Nellis Air Force Base, Nevada, on March 9, 2022, for a Red Flag-Nellis 22-2 mission.** US Air Force/William Lewis

requirements. It's a complex, convoluted decision-making process to reach that end state.

"Also, we can't take away all a squadron's jets at any given time. Even when that squadron is at the lowest point of its maintenance phase it needs three aircraft to fly and train its people, so we keep that flow going throughout time. With all squadrons centrally located and owned by the commodore, it allows us to shorten the timelines, so there are a lot of aircraft swaps."

The first aircraft inducted for GCM was the first EA-18G production aircraft delivered to the US Navy in 2007.

Growler Fleet Operations

Discussing the operations of Growler squadrons deployed around the world recently, Commander Dobbs said: "Electronic Attack Squadron 133 (VAQ-133) 'Wizards' is a boat squadron, one that deploys aboard an aircraft carrier, assigned to CVW-9 and the USS *Nimitz* (CVN 68). Its last deployment started on the trailing edge of the COVID pandemic and was the first back-to-normal deployment undertaken by one of our squadrons.

"The Wizards spent a lot of time operating in the South China Sea area, where a lot of Chinese ships and aircraft were underway, primarily to look at what we were doing. We of course were looking at what they were doing. The air wing spent a lot of time intercepting Chinese aircraft and ships and interacted with them. Ninety-nine percent of the time, the conduct of the Chinese pilots during those engagements was very professional. But the People's Liberation Army has become a little more aggressive in sending aircraft out which has noticeably changed post COVID."

On March 28, 2022, six Growler aircraft assigned to Electronic Attack Squadron 134 (VAQ-134) 'Garudas' arrived at Spangdahlem Air Base, Germany. VAQ-134 is an expeditionary Growler squadron, one that deploys to a land base and not onboard an aircraft carrier.

Announcing the deployment, Pentagon Press Secretary John Kirby said: "This [deployment] is to bolster readiness, enhance NATO's collective defence posture and further increase air

Right: **An aviation ordnance man inspects the fin integrity of a missile on an EA-18G Growler assigned to Electronic Attack Squadron 131 (VAQ-131) 'Lancers'.** US Navy/Mass Communication Specialist Jan David De Luna Mercado

Right: **An EA-18G Growler assigned to Electronic Attack Squadron 133 (VAQ-133) 'Wizards' launches from the flight deck of the aircraft carrier USS *Abraham Lincoln* (CVN 72).** US Navy/Mass Communication Specialist Clayton Wren

integration capabilities with our allied and partner nations."

About 240 personnel, including maintainers and pilots, accompanied the aircraft to Spangdahlem from where they flew missions in support of eastern flank deterrence and defence.

"Following Russia's invasion of Ukraine, the JCS requested the IRF squadron deploy along with F-35s and tankers," said Cdr Dobbs. "It took 56 hours from notification to the aircraft touching down at Spangdahlem. Of course, we had seen the way the wind was blowing, and we had some equipment ready to go.

"VAQ-134 was supported by five C-5M and seven C-17s, making it the largest squadron movement we had ever undertaken, because there was no navy infrastructure at Spangdahlem, for example ground support equipment (GSE). We had to move a lot of gear in a short timeline and had insufficient time to deploy any MMS. Instead, we moved 35 Conex boxes to Spangdahlem, each full of gear for setting up a maintenance facility. ALQ-99 jammer pods, not resident in the EUCOM theatre, were also moved to Spangdahlem.

"The squadron and its aircraft were operating within 72 hours of arrival at Spangdahlem from where all missions were flown. VAQ-134 conducted two flights a day, a section a piece, so four jets in total, a much higher operating tempo than normal.

"Flying from Spangdahlem to the Baltic meant long missions yet the squadron provided 16 hours of coverage each day. Six aircraft were deployed, one extra to the squadron's normal complement, with sufficient components to keep all six operating.

"VAQ-134 was the first squadron to deploy the electronic attack capability to northern NATO states. There were two reasons, the ALQ-99 jamming pod causes EMI issues, so there was hesitancy in the past to do that, and there haven't been many carriers deployed to northern Europe. Consequently, we haven't had an electronic attack capability presence there for a long time. Sentiments have changed. VAQ-134 created an appetite for the aircraft's electronic attack capability from NATO members.

Below: **An EA-18G Growler, assigned to Electronic Attack Squadron 133 (VAQ-133) 'Wizards' makes an arrested landing on the flight deck of the aircraft carrier USS *Abraham Lincoln* (CVN 72).** US Navy/Mass Communication Specialist Seaman Julia Brockman

"Since VAQ-134 returned home from Spangdahlem, three boat squadrons, VAQ-137 (USS *Harry S Truman*), VAQ-140 (USS *George H W Bush*) and VAQ-142 (USS *Gerald Ford*), have all operated in the northern Europe AOR, so a lot more Growlers involved in that AOR.

"VAQ-134 didn't remain at Spangdahlem for a full six months, and once back at Whidbey Island, the CVWP swapped the IRF squadron. We left enough non-permanent infrastructure equipment behind to enable a squadron deploying in the future to fall-in even quicker.

"The squadron's return was based on three things. One, it's expensive to keep a Growler squadron anywhere. Two, there's a lot of opportunity costs to keeping a Growler squadron deployed. Could the squadron immediately redeploy somewhere else if a situation developed? Three, VAQ-134's deployment was a provocation response. Putin acted; we acted by deploying a lot of aircraft to Europe. Did Putin's action stop? Did Putin's action escalate, or did it de-escalate? We waited to see what happened and nothing really changed, it was a steady state. So why keep all the assets in Europe spending a lot of money, with all the opportunity costs when Putin didn't change his behaviour? The provocation response style stalled out, which is not a bad thing.

"Daily flight operations at Spangdahlem involved a morning go and an afternoon go, both to provide a show of presence, and offensive counter air. Missions involved flying to the Baltic region or to Poland down to the area around Lask, and then back home. There was also a separate go every day of two aircraft which conducted joint training with US Air Forces Europe aircraft, coalition training with the Germans, and dets up to Denmark and Finland. VAQ-134 also flew missions with F-35As assigned to the 388th Fighter Wing which were also deployed to Spangdahlem. When a Growler operates with F-35s it provides a layered effect, both aircraft enhance the other's operational capability."

VAQ-131 'Lancers' is another expeditionary Growler squadron and was the first such squadron to deploy to the PACOM AOR post COVID. In October 2022, the Lancers deployed to Misawa Air Base, Japan, for a

of Korea forces in country and at Andersen Air Force Base, Guam. VAQ-131 also made a series of detachments to Kadena Air Base, Okinawa and Marine Corps Air Station Iwakuni, Japan and notably operated with, not aboard, two deployed carriers underway in the South China Sea.

Addressing the size of an expeditionary squadron, Cdr Dobbs said: "In terms of assigned personnel, expeditionary squadrons are a little bit larger than boat squadrons, because there are certain things that already exist on the boat that don't exist in an expeditionary unit, for example a security component. We have as many as 220 in an expeditionary squadron compared to 180 in a fully-manned boat squadron.

Left: **An EA-18G Growler assigned to Electronic Attack Squadron 133 (VAQ-133) 'Wizards' launches from the flight deck of the aircraft carrier USS *Abraham Lincoln* (CVN 72).** US Navy/Mass Communication Specialist Clayton Wren

Middle: **Assigned to the Wizards, an EA-18G Growler launches from the flight deck of the aircraft carrier USS *Abraham Lincoln* (CVN 72) underway conducting routine operations in the US 3rd Fleet area of operations.** US Navy/Mass Communication Specialist Michael Singley

Below: **An EA-18G Growler assigned to the 'Wizards' of Electronic Attack Squadron 133 (VAQ-133) launches from the flight deck of the aircraft carrier USS *Abraham Lincoln* (CVN 72).** US Navy/Mass Communication Specialist Michael Singley

six-month deployment. Misawa served as the squadron's main operating base but also as the hub supporting detachments to Osan Air Base in the Republic of Korea, and Andersen Air Force Base, Guam.

During VAQ-131's deployment a group of five Russian naval ships sailed south along the Pacific side of Japan into the East China Sea, and north into the Sea of Japan. Throughout the transit, the Lancers shadowed the Russian flotilla.

Also notable was the squadron's time at Osan. It was the first deployment made by an EA-18G expeditionary squadron to the Republic of Korea since the COVID pandemic. During its time in the Republic of Korea, the Lancers exercised with Republic

Left: **During June 2022, the USS *Abraham Lincoln* Strike Group was on a scheduled deployment in the US 7th Fleet area of operations to enhance interoperability through alliances and partnerships while serving as a ready-response force in support of a free and open Indo-Pacific region.** US Navy/Mass Communication Specialist Seaman Kassandra Alanis

Below: **Two shooters see off an EA-18G Growler, assigned to VAQ-133 from the flight deck of the aircraft carrier USS *Abraham Lincoln* (CVN 72) while underway in the Philippine Sea during a scheduled deployment in the US 7th Fleet area of operations.** US Navy/Mass Communication Specialist Michael Singley

"Expeditionary squadrons are jointly manned by US Navy and US Air Force personnel, consequently each unified combatant command submits its requirements and wing staff determines the schedule of where each squadron is going, and we always have a squadron in PACOM. Currently CENTCOM has a 1.0 requirement, 1.0 denotes a requirement to have one squadron deployed there for 12 months of the year; 1.5 denotes a requirement to have a squadron deployed there for 12 months of the year and another squadron there for six months of the year. EUCOM's current requirement is 1.0 and PACOM is 2.0. All requirements can be filled either by an expeditionary squadron or a boat squadron.

"Given the 2.0 requirement in PACOM, we always have a squadron deployed, currently an expeditionary squadron, supported by a hub and spoke system for logistics and maintenance. The core location is Misawa Air Base with the deployed aircraft present at the Japanese base for less than 50% of the deployment timeline. A logistics footprint remains in place, and we have what we call a DANOP det from the Fleet Readiness Center which uses box containers as mobile maintenance facilities. The det conducts all intermediate level maintenance on the aircraft deployed to Misawa including component, composite, wheel, and tyre repairs: all the elements that the squadron cannot do.

"The big difference between an expeditionary vice a boat squadron is the expeditionary squadrons get a lot of tasking from the Joint Chiefs of Staff J3 Operations directorate. Ultimately, they decide where the packages go.

SCORPIONS

Mark Ayton spoke with Electronic Attack Squadron 132's executive officer, Commander Nathaniel Michael. His command is one of five active-duty EA-18G expeditionary squadrons.

AFTER ELECTRONIC ATTACK Squadron 132 (VAQ-132) 'Scorpions' returned to Naval Air Station Whidbey Island from deployment in October 2021, it was due to accept jets that were new to the squadron. Five aircraft configured with the Growler Capability Modification (GCM) and loaded with H16 software were accepted during the maintenance phase.

The autumn of 2021 was a busy time for VAQ-132. The squadron deployed its GCM aircraft with its maintenance department to Naval Air Station Fallon, Nevada to support the Growler Tactics Instructor course run by HAVOC, the Airborne Electronic Attack Weapons School.

In November, VAQ-132 successfully completed the first AGM-88 HARM firings by GCM H16 Growler aircraft assigned to a fleet squadron. VAQ-132 fired two HARM missiles in the W-237 operating area over the Pacific Ocean near Whidbey Island. Launching a set number of missiles is a

requirement for deployment as part of a squadron's normal NCAA expenditure, leading up to deployment.

Commander Michael explained: "It's an end-to-end test, demonstrating that our ordnance team can successfully load the missiles and our mission planners can plan, and the aircrew can complete the firing."

Nellis Deployments

In April 2022, the Scorpions deployed to Nellis Air Force Base to participate in Neptune Hawk, a joint air interoperability exercise hosted by the US Air Force at Nellis and involving high-end scenarios. It is designed to maintain readiness and evaluate employment capabilities in a realistic training environment.

Commenting, Cdr Michael said VAQ-132 did not complete any Growler only events during Neptune Hawk. "Our taskings were issued by the exercise director to meet his requirements. We led a couple of events. Our training officer and our ops officer both got their mission commander qualification for which they led the mission planning, the event and the debrief," he said.

Neptune Hawk involved F-35 Lightning II fighters, a type that EA-18G Growler aircrew operate with on a regular basis. But what does that involve for both the EA-18G crews and the F-35 pilots? Commenting, Cdr Michael said: "We're trying to increase their survivability. However much we can contribute to that is a bonus, so getting them close

enough to targets, getting them to confuse the enemy's surface-to-air radars, just enough to get them to where they can be more lethal. We're usually behind them for the most part loaded with ALQ-99s. We provide kinetic suppression with HARM missiles when we can get close enough to the fight to employ the weapons. When protecting F-35s, our alignment is crucial especially with the newer, more capable radars, when we're particularly effective with our jammers."

Red Flag 22-3 in July 2022 was the squadron's first large exercise in its work-up cycle in preparation for its 2023 deployment. More than 20 units and 2,300 participants took part. It was the first iteration of Red Flag-Nellis that featured

Below: **An EA-18G Growler assigned to Electronic Attack Squadron 132 (VAQ-132) takes off for a Red Flag mission at Nellis Air Force Base, Nevada, on March 15, 2023.** US Air Force/ Senior Airman Zachary Rufus

the first, dedicated fifth-generation 65th Aggressor Squadron.

Discussing the advent of dedicated F-35 aggressors in Red Flag, Colonel Jared Hutchinson, 414th Combat Training Squadron commander said: "The aggressor force will be unleashed as they refine threat replication, apply advanced threats and jamming capabilities, and increase threat capabilities to maximise training in non-permissive environments. The airspace is much different with almost twice as much fight airspace and inclusion of neighbouring airspace opportunities to optimise blue and red force tactics."

Red Flag 22-3 also featured extended night operations, enhanced combat search and rescue scenarios, and a much bigger battle space. Scenarios provided the most true-to-life training experience, designed to prepare airmen to face pacing challenges in the Pacific and elsewhere.

In addition to VAQ-132, other participants included US Navy F-35C Lightning IIs, US Air Force B-1Bs, F-15Es, F-22s, F-35As, HC-130Js, an RC-135, and MQ-9s. The complex tactical problem sets posed by the aggressor force were tough to overcome but gave the blue force realistic combat experience in an advanced training environment.

Right: **EA-18G Growler BuNo 166858/NL540, VAQ-132's CAG-bird, seen at Nellis Air Force Base, Nevada, on March 20, 2023.** US Air Force/ William Lewis

Below: **An EA-18G Growler assigned to VAQ-132 loaded with AGM-88 HARM missiles takes off for a Red Flag mission at Nellis Air Force Base, Nevada.** US Air Force/ Senior Airman Zachary Rufus

540
Scorpions
NAVY

544
LT JACOB BISHOP
"CASKET"
LT DOUG RENEAU
"SUNNY D"
-132

Pre-deployment Work-Up

As part of an expeditionary squadron's deployment work-up it must complete two integrated training events within a year of deploying. The Scorpions' first such event was Exercise Red Flag 23-2 at Nellis which involved Israeli F-35A Adir fighters and Boeing 707 tankers. According to Cdr Michael, the training conducted with the Israeli participants was effective.

As part of its work-up, a Growler squadron follows a training routine called the Electronic Warfare Advanced Readiness Program or EWARP. Ground school started at Whidbey in January comprising classroom training and simulator events. Flight operations from Whidbey began at the beginning of February which was followed by a

two-week detachment to Naval Air Station Fallon in late February.

VAQ-132's second pre-deployment integrated training event was Northern Edge 23-1 operating from Joint Base Elmendorf-Richardson near Anchorage, Alaska. Northern Edge is a high-end, large scale joint exercise. The Scorpions conducted a lot of long-range missions across the Joint Pacific Alaska Range Complex, a 65,000 square mile area of airspace which extends over 800 miles north to south and for 500 miles east to west. Long-range missions also took place over the Gulf of Alaska. VAQ-132 pilots were able to complete aerial refuelling training with US Air Force tankers fitted with an Iron Maiden basket and from some other unfamiliar tanker types. The squadron's involvement was primarily focused on testing tactics, techniques and procedures with some experimentation and proof of concepts.

Around all these events, VAQ-132 has focused on building up the squadron's training and readiness to achieve certification and be ready to deploy.

Cdr Michael said: "Of the many things required, we completed an operational readiness assessment for which aircrew donned MOPP [Mission Oriented Protective Posture] gear and the maintainers completed a launch wearing chemical, biological, and radiological suits and gas masks."

In April 2023, VAQ-132 flew two Growler aircraft to Tyndall Air Force Base in Florida to shoot an AIM-120 AMRAAM missile as part of the Weapon Systems Evaluation Program for air-to-air missiles known as Combat Archer. Cdr Michael said: "At the direction of the air wing commander, we employed a single AIM-120 which is somewhat rare for a Growler squadron, the aircraft is not given the highest priority to employ AIM-120s any more.

"Prior to our deployment we'll do one final three-week period of surge operations which will involve a lot of night-time operations to get our night-time certifications, so our crews are ready for deployment. We will deploy with our own GCM H16-configured aircraft which will be the first such aircraft deployed in theatre. Once we're declared ready to go, we'll deploy within a given period.

"While deployed we will fall under the command of CTF 70 which will issue taskings that we execute to support different exercises at austere, remote locations. Sailors with experience of navy ship deployments are not averse to packing up and going with a limited amount of equipment."

The US Air Force 390th Electronic Control Squadron provides aircrew to the VAQ wing at Whidbey. VAQ-132 has one pilot and one EWO assigned who help fulfil its tasking requirements. ✈

Left: **A VAQ-132 EA-18G Growler on the flight line at Joint Base Elmendorf-Richardson, Alaska, during Exercise Northern Edge 23-1 on May 8, 2023. Northern Edge is a large-scale exercise that focuses on improving interchangeability in operations, techniques, and procedures.** US Navy/Mass Communication Specialist Jen Martinez

Below: **VAQ-132's CAG-bird taxies to the runway at Joint Base Elmendorf-Richardson, Alaska, during Exercise Northern Edge 23-1 on May 8, 2023.** US Navy/Mass Communication Specialist Jen Martinez

STAR
WARRIORS

Mark Ayton spoke with Commander Cameron Dekker, commander of the only US Navy Reserve squadron equipped with the EA-18G Growler.

NOT ONLY IS Electronic Attack Squadron 209 (VAQ-209) 'Star Warriors' a US Navy Reserve Squadron, but it's also the only one equipped with the EA-18G Growler and is an expeditionary squadron. Its primary objective is to provide strategic depth to the active-duty fleet cost effectively. Typically, VAQ-209 deploys on a two-year cycle.

Based at Naval Air Station Whidbey Island, Washington, VAQ-209 has five Growler aircraft assigned, 110 full-time active-duty sailors, and 80 selected reservist sailors who have jobs in the civilian world. The reservists work at the squadron during drill weekends and when the squadron is mobilised. About 90% of the squadron's reservists are located throughout the USA, so a typical drill weekend requires them to travel to Whidbey, which is less than convenient. To ease the burden of travelling to Whidbey for drill weekends, each quarter, the squadron deploys to a location such as Key West, Las Vegas, and New Orleans, for two to three weeks, to complete training exercises. Such detachments provide squadron personnel an opportunity to drill and complete orders.

Prior to joining the EA-18G community, Commander Cameron Dekker served with the US Navy Reserve E-2C Hawkeye squadron based at Naval Air Station New Orleans Joint Reserve Base. Dekker was assigned to the then Carrier Airborne Early Warning Squadron 77 (VAW-77) 'Nightwolves' which flew counter narcotics and illicit trafficking missions in the Caribbean and South America. The squadron was disestablished in March 2013 because of budget cuts, and the Department of Defense's pivotal shift to the Pacific theatre. In 2014, Cdr Dekker applied for a job with VAQ-209, got selected, and went through the full Growler course with VAQ-129. He joined VAQ-209 for a department head tour, then completed a staff tour, and was selected for command. Cdr Dekker served with VAQ-209 full-time

Above:
VAQ-209's CAG-bird, EA-18G BuNo 166895/AF500, fires an AGM-88 High-speed Anti-Radiation Missile. US Navy/ Commander Peter Scheu

Right: **A top-down image of VA-209's CAG-bird loaded with an AGM-88 HARM.** US Navy/ Commander Peter Scheu

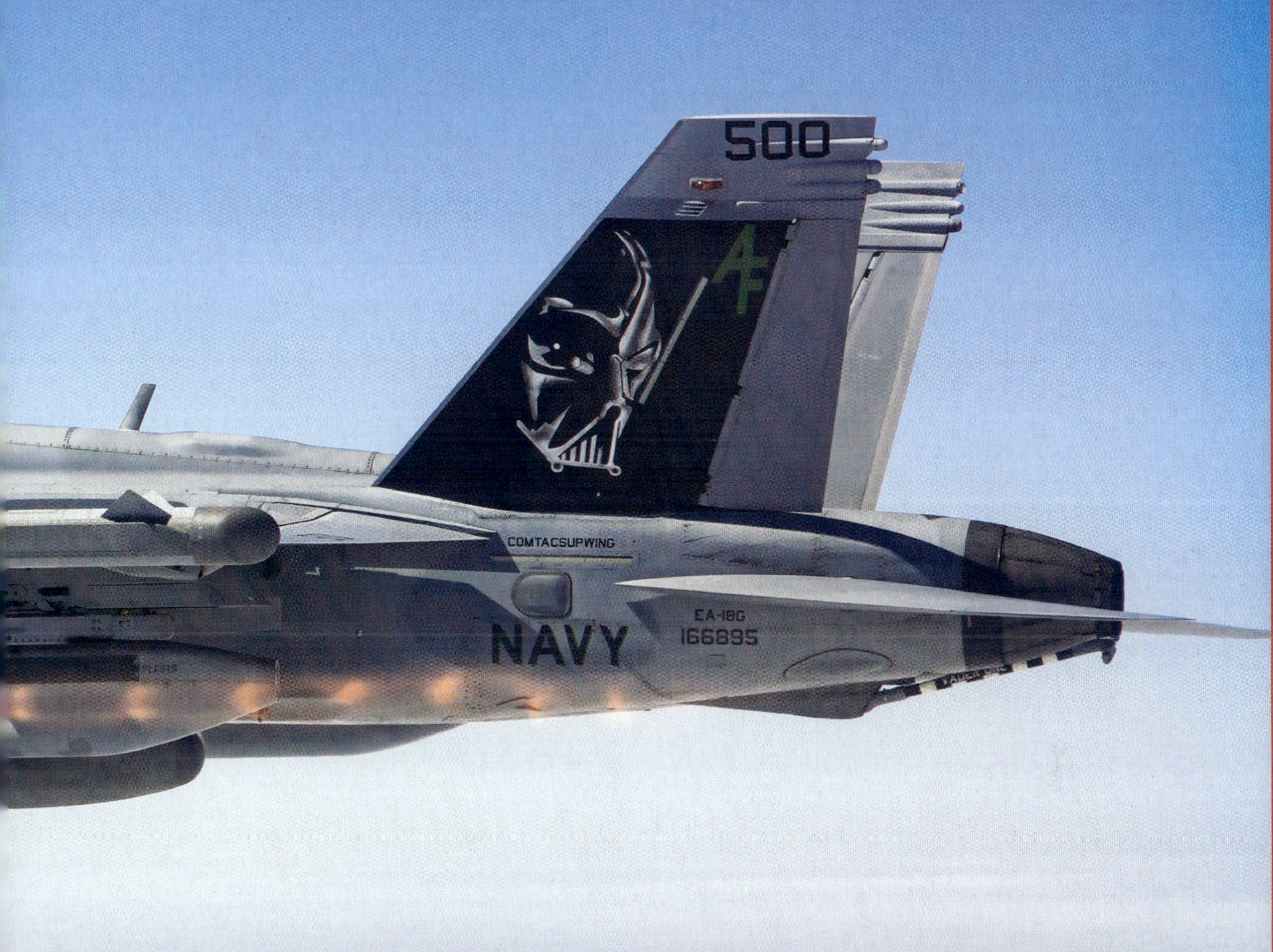
500
COMTACSUPWING
NAVY
EA-18G
166895

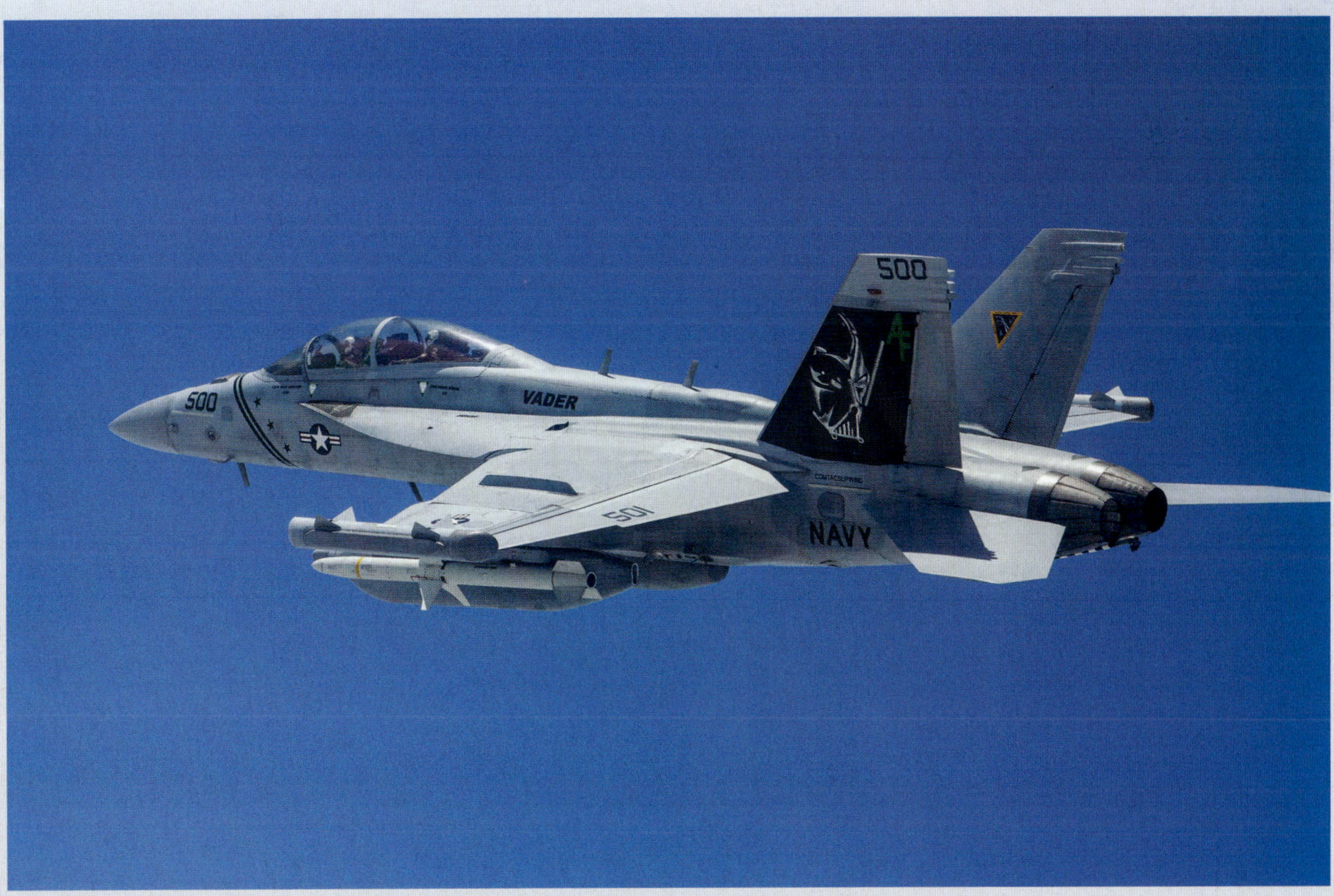
500
500
VADER
501
NAVY

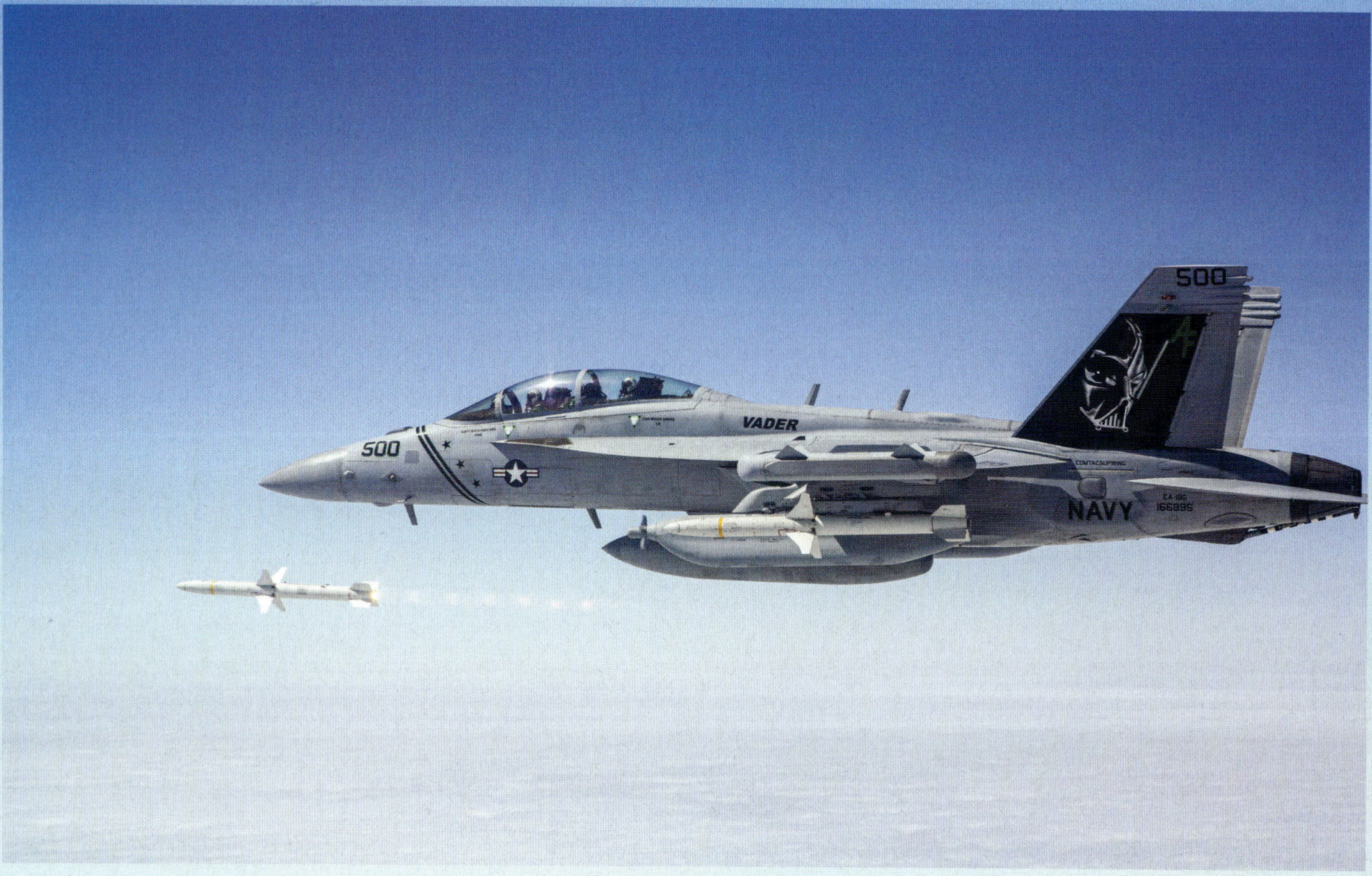
500
VADER
500
NAVY

500
CAPT BILLY FRASER
CAG
CAPT GEOFFREY HUGHES
DCAG

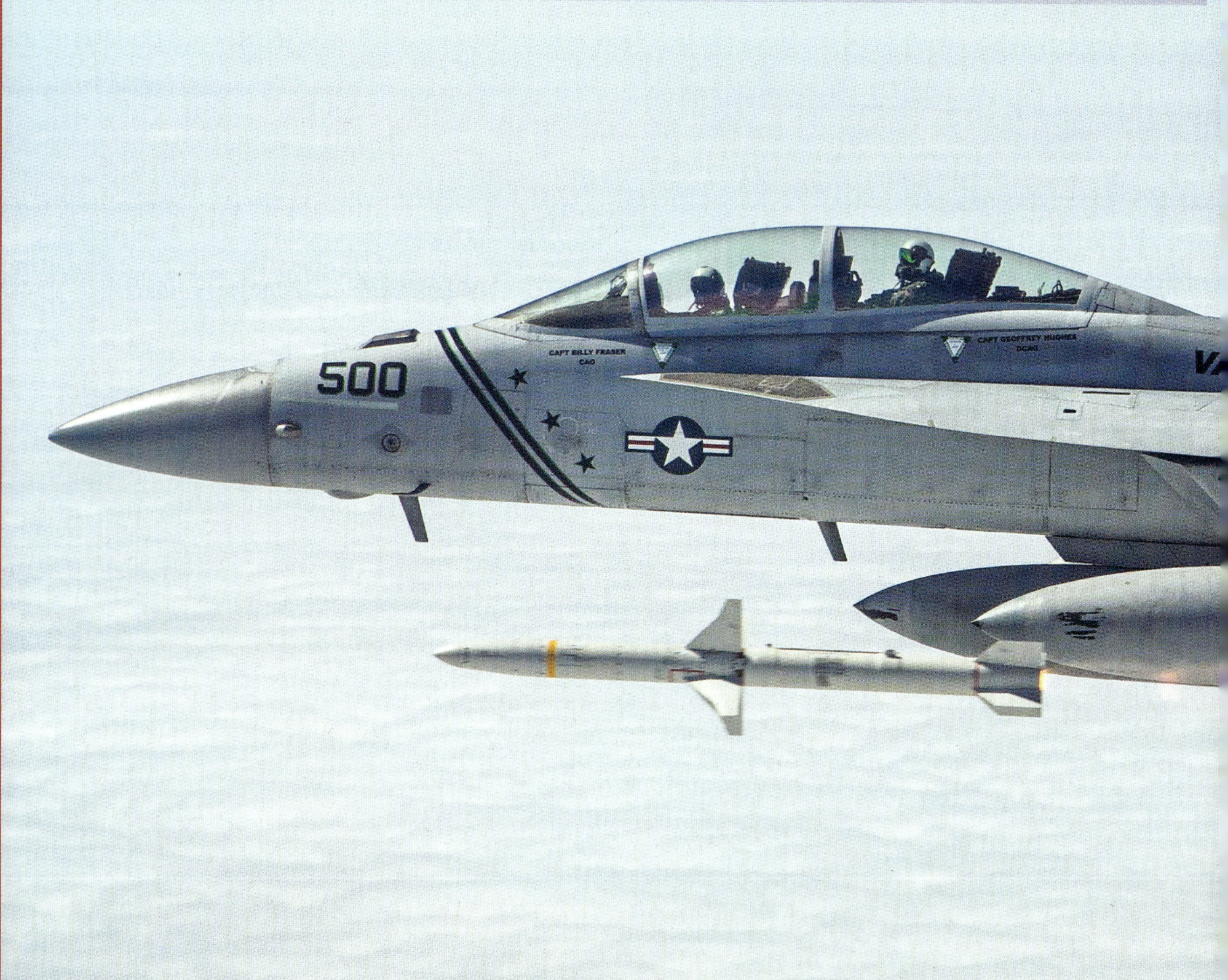

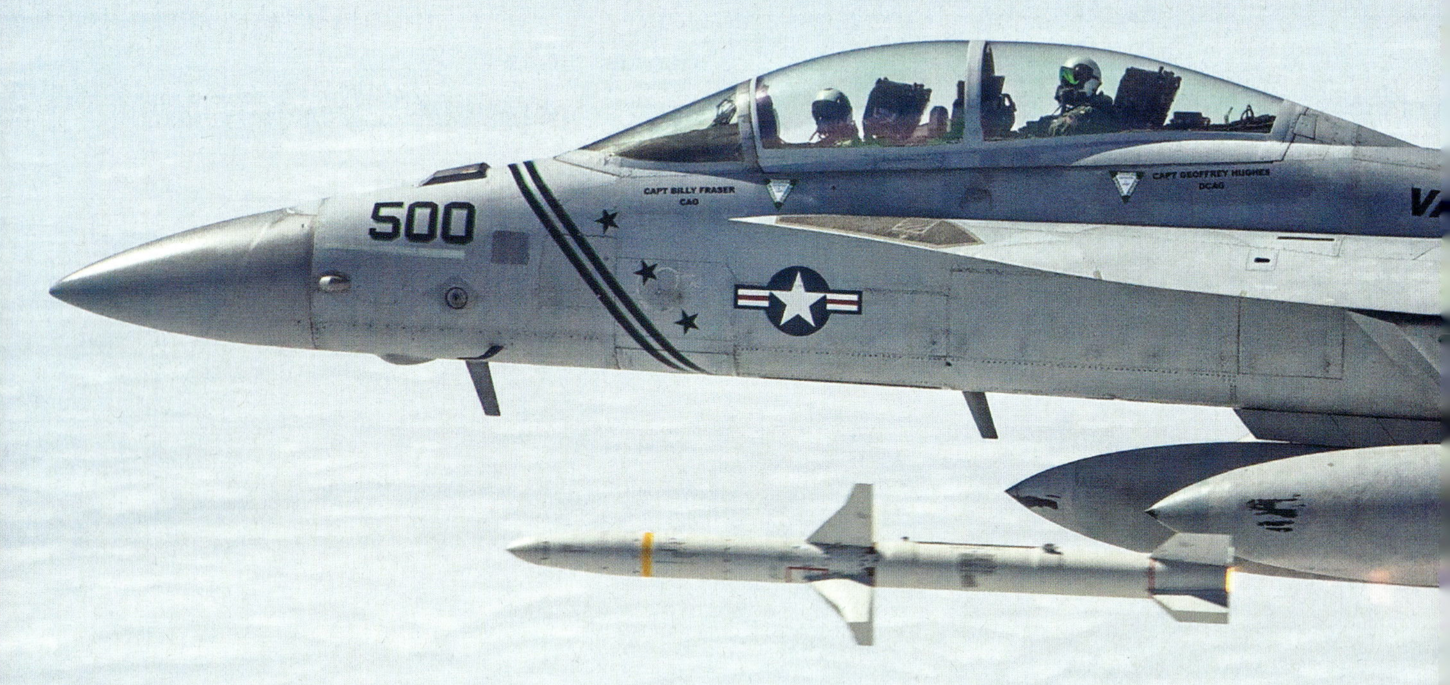

from 2014, and currently has over 1,000 hours in the EA-18G Growler.

Discussing the squadron's sailors, Cdr Dekker said: "Except for one, our selective reservist pilots fly for Delta, American, United, FedEx, or UPS. Our electronic warfare officers work for consulting firms, government agencies, and agencies on base that support the electronic attack community."

Mission Set, Training and Work-ups

The requirements for VAQ-209 to deploy are the same as an active-duty expeditionary squadron.

Discussing the squadron's deployment work-up, Cdr Dekker said: "In a year that we mobilise [deploy], the active-duty sailors carry a lot of the load. We have about 110 full-time sailors who carry out the same workload as an active-duty expeditionary squadron with 170 people. For deployment, our selective reservists must organise getting time off with their employers for the purpose of completing the same workup as an active-duty

squadron; same wickets, flight hours, and motions for getting certified to deploy.

"Pilots must maintain a minimum currency of five hours in 90 days. Each aircrew must fly the exact same number of hours as an active-duty counterpart: 100 hours for pilots and 48 hours for an EWO. Everybody in the squadron gets 100-plus hours per year.

"Managing that with all the other requirements on the squadron requires a lot of planning and a lot of communication to enable the sailors to plan their lives and discuss with their

employers the demands that are going to be asked of them for a 12-to-18-month mobilisation period. Communication must be constant. Generally, if we are going to deploy, we get the word out, and then organise the work-up schedule with the wing.

"The work-up includes tactical refresher training in accordance with the EWARP syllabus, shooting HARM or air-to-air missiles as a benchmark test of the squadron's ability to fire and employ weapons, air-to-air training, and a couple of large force exercises.

"Each pilot must spend 100 hours practicing different skill sets to gain points which are accumulated to get their deployment certification. For example, flying with ALQ-99 pods for a certain number of flights, turning the pods on for a certain number of flights, and flying with NVGs for a certain number of night-time hours. Monitoring the criteria and tallying the points from each mission falls to the operations officer, which help demonstrate the squadron is ready.

"Prior to deploying to Misawa, Japan, VAQ-209 participated in two integrated training exercises: Northern Lightning 2021 at Volk Field, Wisconsin in August 2021 which featured F-16s, F-22s and F-35s, tanker support and AWACS, and Red Flag-Alaska in May 2022.

"We used the January 2022 edition of Exercise in Sentry Aloha in Hawaii to prevent the skills required for coordinating tankers, air lift, and cargo movements, from atrophying. In June 2022 we deployed to Misawa, Japan for a three-month mobilisation, a Navy Reserve term for deployment.

"We had to plan-out everything in such a way that the pilots and EWOs maintained their currencies because every task has periodicity, which expire after a certain number of days.

"The more difficult part is planning for our selected reservists and the civilian pilots. While in the periodicity window we got refresher training and realigned the dates beyond the end of the deployment period. It's a constant race to show we're ready in green all the way through without letting any of the apples fall off the truck.

"Another difficult aspect comes about when a reserve squadron is mobilised. It creates significant administrative and legal paperwork and requires plenty of lead time for medical screening."

Below: **The supersonic AGM-88 HARM is powered by a solid-propellant, dual thrust rocket motor, weighs approximately 800lb, and measures 164in in length.** US Navy/Commander Peter Scheu

Right: US Navy/ Commander Peter Scheu

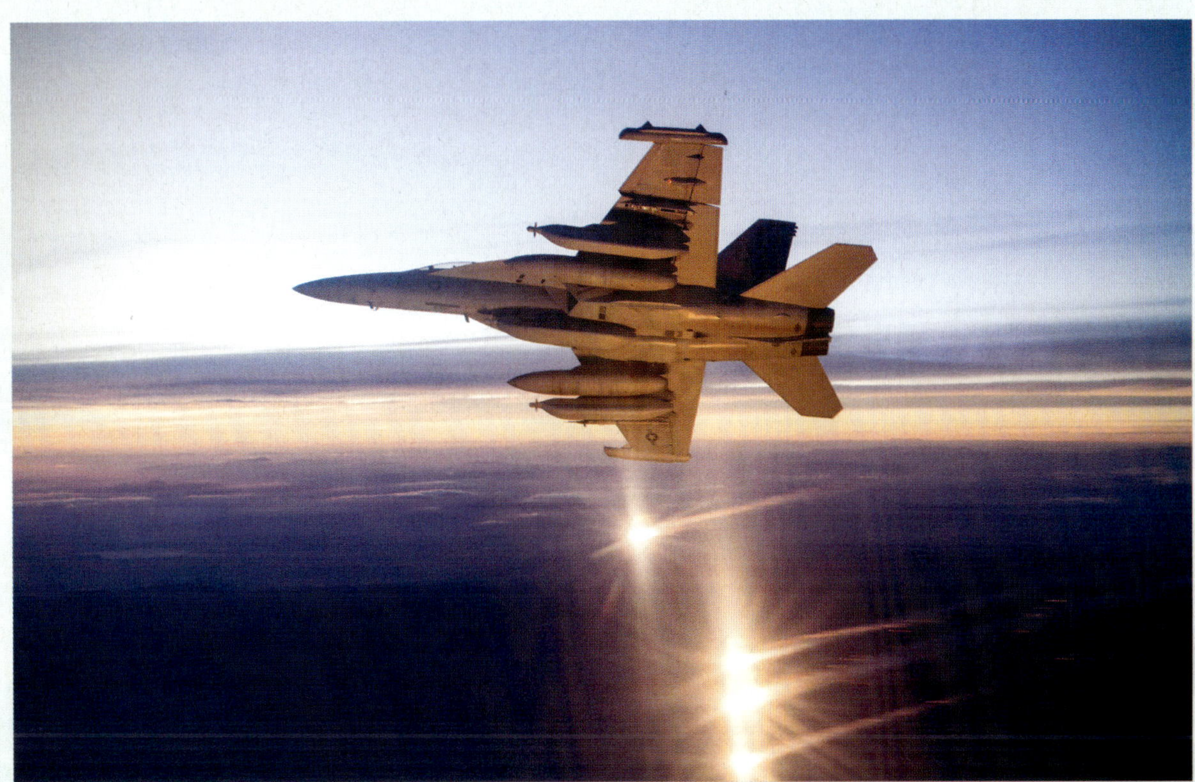

Misawa 2022

When VAQ-209 deployed to Misawa in June 2022, it did not fly its assigned aircraft to Japan. Untypically and for the first time, the squadron took custody of aircraft from the squadron already there. The move involved a huge airlift of lots of people. This was not the scenario on the squadron's return to Whidbey, as Cdr Dekker explained: "We flew the aircraft back. This involved lots of planning and lots of maintenance. It took about a week to get back to Whidbey because of downtime required after flying long legs. For example, Guam to Hawaii is a nine-hour flight with tanking. It required piddle packs and packed meals, so it's no fun."

During the Misawa deployment, VAQ-209 demonstrated the flexibility of an expeditionary squadron by sending detachments to Iwakuni, Osan, and Guam, largely as a deterrent to whatever was going on in the region at the time. Each detachment was tasked by Commander Task Force 70, who is the admiral for Carrier Strike Group 5 based on the USS *George Washington* (CVN 73), who also had charge of VAQ-209.

Cdr Dekker continued: "In Japan we were flying missions in support of the Unit Deployment Program and integration missions with the US Air Force F-16 squadrons based at Misawa and the JASDF F-35 squadrons also based there. Similarly, when we operated from Osan in

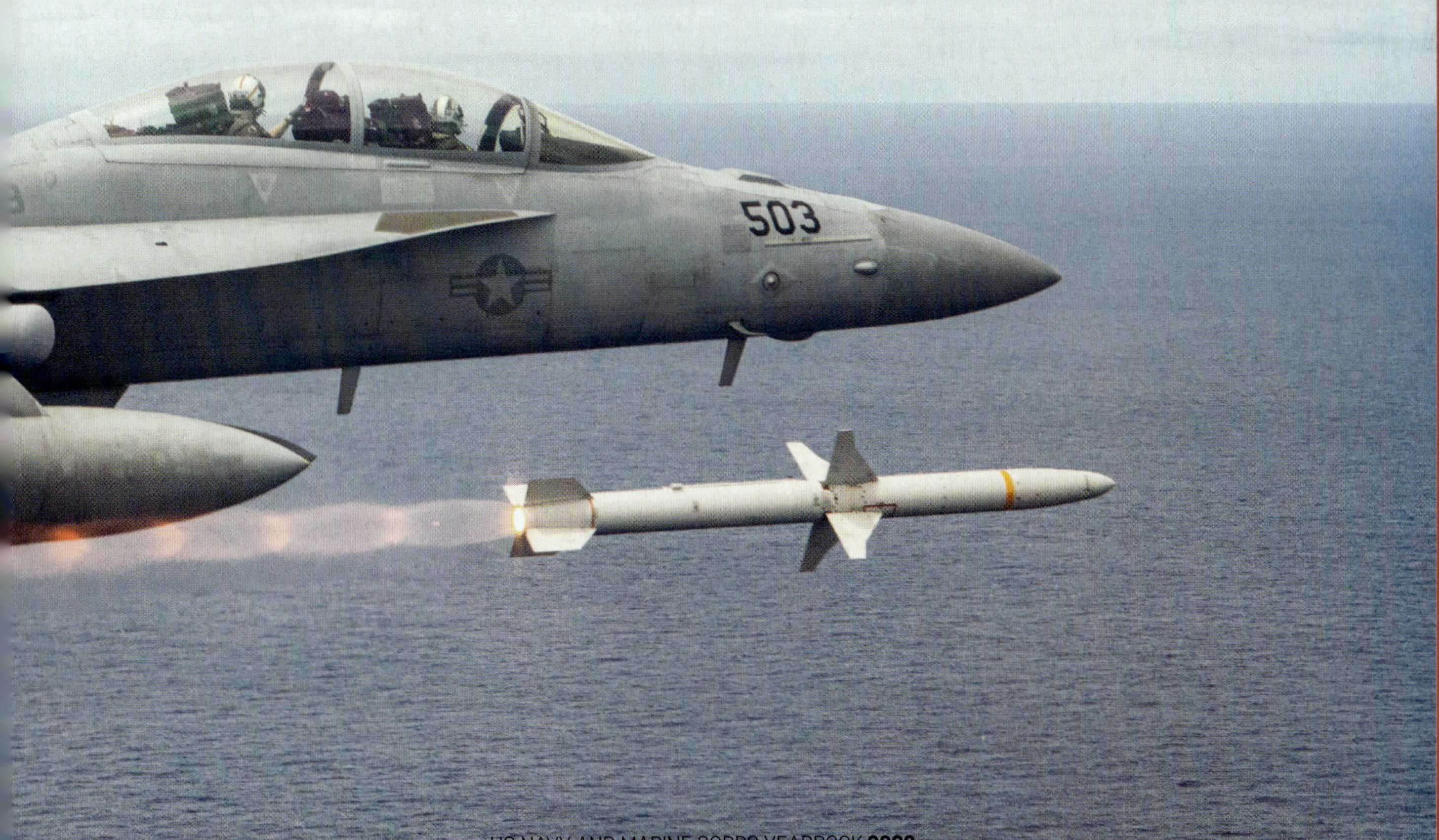

VAQ-209's CAG-bird Growler leads a formation of two F/A-18C Hornets assigned to Strike Fighter Squadron 204 (VFA-204) and two F-5N Tigers assigned to Fighter Composite Squadron (VFC-13). All three squadrons are assigned to the Navy Reserve's Tactical Support Wing. US Navy/Commander Peter Scheu

the Republic of Korea, we flew integration missions with the resident A-10 and F-16 squadrons.

"In June 2023, VAQ-209 was conducting flight operations at Whidbey Island in support of unit level training missions. These were flown to keep the squadron's selected reservist aircrews current with the Growler's mission sets, suppression of enemy air defences, electronic attack, communication jamming, and basic fighter manoeuvring.

"For day-to-day flight operations eight officers serving as department heads run everything on the squadron, including many collateral duties. When the selected reservist pilots hold duty on the squadron, their primary job is to fly and work as a department head which keeps them involved in that department's activity, which helps them to assume the role from a full-time colleague when mobilised."

Road to Deployment

In August, VAQ-209 deployed to Savannah International Airport, home of the Georgia Air National Guard-run Combat Readiness Training Center to participate in Exercise Century Savannah. The Star Warriors flew integration missions with F-16s and F-35s, supported by tankers and US Navy Arleigh Burke-class guided-missile destroyers underway in the western Atlantic.

Century Savannah counted as a large force integrated exercise.

After a short turnaround at Whidbey, VAQ-209 deployed to Naval Air Station Point Mugu, California to shoot AGM-88 HARM missiles. This is an annual requirement for an Electronic Attack Squadron.

Discussing VAQ-209's deployment to Misawa, Japan in June 2022, Cdr Dekker explained how an electronic attack squadron was deployed to Spangdahlem Air Base at the time. He said: "That affected when the squadron already deployed to Misawa was to be replaced. VAQ-209 was asked if it could go early. It was a big ask for a reserve squadron. Fortunately, we were given enough lead time to deploy to Misawa early to enable the squadron in Japan at the time to return home a little bit earlier than expected.

"In April 2023, we deployed to Nellis to participate in Exercise Neptune Eagle. This is an exercise organised by the US Air Force Weapon School which supplements the Weapons School Integration phase at the end of the six-month course. Neptune Eagle focuses on fifth generation integration and electronic attack and includes other US Air Force assets."

by using Expeditionary Advanced Base Operations. LtGen Iiams directed Col Purcell to remain focused on training WTIs who can prepare the MAGTF for the full range of military operations ranging from insurgents to those of peer competitors, primarily China, and not make the course exclusive to Expeditionary Advanced Base Operations.

Col Purcell said that after careful consideration, he opted to provide students with more time to read and incorporate the lessons by adjusting the length of their working day. He also opted to change the course content to include threat systems that peer adversaries such as China might use against US forces in any conflict. He said: "My impression was that the course was still heavily tailored to former Soviet Union systems. So, we created a robust study guide on advanced Chinese and Russian threats so the students can learn which ones are the most lethal and which ones they would most likely encounter in conflict. At the start of each course, we test the students on MAGTF operations, followed by a test on advanced threats. Additionally, we've made a concerted effort to ensure those threats are replicated in the flying phase. Typically, peer threat scenarios are based on how we envision having to fight in the future, with more focus on naval integration. Maritime

strike is now incorporated in the TACAIR specifics and the FINEX."

Col Purcell explained three unique things about MAWTS-1: "All our instructors, for the most part, are hand selected from amongst the best. We control the syllabus. So, if we see a changing threat environment and need to update any aspect of the period of instruction, as the commanding officer I can direct any one of my department or division heads to make a change to the course so that fleet operators don't get surprised if they were to go up against a new enemy threat. There are not many

places in the military where the authority and the ability to change and update a course lies with an O-6 commander, but at MAWTS-1 it is. Furthermore, by having hand selected instructors, the course is run in a far better way than if I tried to micromanage every aspect of it."

Student Preparation

The course has a specific set of aircrew prerequisites for each type-model-series of aircraft, helicopter, tiltrotor, or unmanned aerial system flown by the US Marine Corps.

For an F/A-18 pilot to attend the WTI, he or she must have graduated from either

Above: **An MV-22B Osprey tiltrotor prepares to take off during a ground threat reaction drill at Marine Corps Air Station Yuma, Arizona, during WTI 2-23.** US Marine Corps/ LCpl Alejandro Fernandez

Left: **A US Navy MH-60S Seahawk assigned to HSC-21 based at Naval Air Station North Island at a landing zone at Marine Corps Air Station Camp Pendleton, California, during a command-and-control mission in the FINEX of WTI 2-23.** US Marine Corps/LCpl Ruben Padilla

TOPGUN (the US Navy's fighter weapons school) or the Marine Division Tactics Course (MDTC), a one-month event run by MAWTS-1 twice a year at Miramar in the spring and Beaufort in the summer.

Explaining, Major Luke Stephenson, an F/A-18 instructor pilot with MAWTS-1 said: "They are fully qualified as a four-ship, division lead, and as a mission commander. They have a high-level working knowledge of the aircraft and its associated systems."

Fellow KC-130 instructor pilot, Major Brian Kursawe added: "KC-130 students are experts in individual missions conducted by the KC-130J. Our job is to get them to apply that to more complex missions and integrate with other platforms and agencies, often those they have not previously encountered. These are important aspects because the KC-130J tends to operate alone, long distances away from the rest of the MAGTF.

"We emphasise attention to communications and communications pathways, integrating threats, planning for threats, and managing risk to make them better MAGTF planners and KC-130 mission commanders when they get

Above: **US Marines complete the refuelling of an F/A-18D Hornet during aviation delivered ground refuelling operations at Marine Corps Air Station Yuma, Arizona, during WTI 2-23.** US Marine Corps/ Cpl Eric Ramirez

Left: **Aviation delivered ground refuelling operations is a standard procedure conducted by US Marine Corps aviation squadrons and is one event undertaken during the seven-week Weapons and Tactics Instructors course.** US Marine Corps/Cpl Eric Ramirez

back to the fleet. During the WTI course, students fly missions across the KC-130J's mission set including aerial refuelling, air delivery, aviation delivered ground refuelling and combat assault transport."

MV-22B instructor pilot, Major Zachary Behler said: "We put our students in scenarios that they don't do frequently encounter in fleet operations. Our goal is to train them as MAGTF planners and integrators so they understand all functions of marine aviation and can integrate all assets in the respective air and ground combat elements of a MAGTF in order to facilitate and complete the mission.

"Most of our students are familiar with most of the rotary wing types based on their experiences from deployment work-up and execution, but they don't have a whole lot of fixed wing integration experience, so we like to expose our students to that as much as we can, during the WTI course. One example is called the long-range airfield seizure. The MV-22s take-off from Yuma and fly to an airfield located hundreds of miles away, conduct the seizure operation and return to Yuma. The objective is to get to the airfield and back using the MV-22's organic fuel payload and fuel uploaded from KC-130Js and either US Air Force KC-135s or KC-46s. The WTI 2-23 mission was supported by a

Left: **A UH-1Y Venom crew chief assigned to Marine Light Attack Helicopter Squadron 167 (HMLA-167) participates in a close air support exercise at Wiss Flats Airfield, near Chocolate Mountains, California, during WTI 2-23.** US Marine Corps/LCpl Dakota Hungerford

KC-46. What we don't want to rely upon is any sort of ground refuelling. The airfield seizure operation staged for WTI 2-23 involved US Marine Corps F/A-18s and F-35s, US Navy EA-18G Growlers and a US Air Force C-17 Globemaster. It's generally conducted in a GPS-denied combat environment that really opens a student's purview of the support assets available to them, and the more difficult mission sets that they might have to execute in a future conflict."

As part of the student's preparation, instructors from MAWTS-1 visit a pilot's squadron, whatever the type, to evaluate not just the student, but the process used by that squadron to certify pilots at all levels of the US Marine Corps' combat training programme.

A visiting MAWTS-1 instructor can recommend a pilot for WTI participation, which is ultimately signed off by the pilot's commanding officer. By visiting a squadron, an instructor is given a chance to determine whether a student is ready for the gruelling demands of the course. The instructor's judgement is crucial to the student and the course. The course is tough with an historical rate of failure between three to 5%. Consequently, MAWTS-1 staff do not want students to arrive at MAWTS-1 who are not ready. The process of visiting squadrons and preparing students to attend the course takes about 12 months: an instructor will spend one month preparing, and two months conducting each WTI course during which time they remain unavailable to visit potential students at their squadrons.

Departments

MAWTS-1 is organised into departments, each responsible for a specific function; the rotary wing and tactical aircraft (TACAIR) departments are further organised into divisions, each responsible for a specific mission set and aircraft type.

The air officer course is designed to produce officers who control all the forward air controllers in a regiment and orchestrates the integration of aviation, fires, and assault support with the ground scheme of manoeuvre in a combat scenario.

The air officer course is usually taken by pilots with experience of working as a forward air controller with a ground unit, some of whom previously attended WTI as a pilot.

Each course usually graduates 12 air officers who get posted to a variety of non-flying jobs classed as DIFDEN (duty involving flight operations denied)

Below: **A UH-1Y Venom helicopter lands during a battle drill exercise at K-9 Village located in the Yuma Proving Ground, Arizona during WTI 2-23.** US Marine Corps/ Cpl Jaye Townsend

billets with Marine Expeditionary Units; either of the Expeditionary Warfare Training Groups; and in some cases, to a rifle regimental headquarters or a division.

Aviation Command, Control and Communications (C3) is one of the largest departments with nearly 25% of the course footprint comprising enlisted and officer students who train to conduct the following functions.

- Tactical Air Control Party (TACP) provides terminal attack control for close air support to career enlisted JTACs and pilots qualified as forward air controllers. All graduates are aviation integrators in support of the MAGTF.
- Tactical Air Operations Centre (TAOC) provides air surveillance and control of aircraft and surface-to-air weapons for anti-air warfare in support of the MAGTF.
- Marine Air Traffic Control Mobile Team (MMT) provides air traffic control to aircraft in austere and/or improved landing environments.
- Direct Air Support Center (DASC), the principal Marine air control agency, provides procedural control and

Above: **A KC-130J crew chief assigned to Marine Aerial Refueler Transport Squadron 234 (VMGR-234) watches over the control panel during an air-delivery mission.** US Marine Corps/LCpl Ruben Padilla

Right: **US Marines assigned to Marine Wing Support Squadron 371 load an M31 arresting gear system for expeditionary airfield operations onto a KC-130J Hercules at Marine Corps Air Station Yuma, Arizona, during WTI 2-23.** US Marine Corps/ Cpl Christopher Hernandez

routing from the operating airfield to the objective area and back.

The C3 department also has a spectrum warfare division which provides a course on cyber, electronic warfare and MAGTF integration. C3 knits all the aviation functions together in support of the mission.

The Aviation Ground Support Department runs a course taken by marines who undertake many roles

that include building airfields, laying AM-2 matting, conducting bulk fuelling of aircraft, providing air base ground defence at forward bases, and ensuring the MAGTF has all the supplies and equipment required to sustain an operation.

Course Phases

The WTI course runs for about seven weeks with three specific phases: academics and flying (each with a generic,

Left: **A US Marine assigned to a Tactical Air Control Party uses a portable lightweight designator rangefinder during a close air support exercise at Wiss Airfield, near Chocolate Mountains, California.** US Marine Corps/ LCpl Alejandro Fernandez

stress for which the MAWTS-1 instructors conduct lectures about the techniques for doing that.

The common component focuses on aspects of a mission that are common to all students in each respective field. By contrast, the specifics component, the smallest component of the academics' phase, provides detailed instruction to all students from a respective type about the aircraft, including sensors and weapons, to gain more expertise.

Flight Phase

In support of the flying phase and before flight operations begin, MAWTS-1 forms a maintenance department comprising hundreds of marines at Yuma from units based around the fleet.

Flight operations last for 21 days, and in contrast to the academic phase, comprises the same three components, though these are conducted in reverse order.

Day one involves an orientation flight followed by three or four days of type-specific flying for the specifics component. For example, CH-53s conduct individual CH-53 tasks such as landing in a restricted visibility scenario or conducting air delivery of equipment.

In the second week of flight operations, the course enters the common component which involves different types operating together. For example, CH-53s fly a long-range raid escorted by AH-1 attack helicopters, stop for fuel at a forward-arming and refuelling point and then go into the objective area, with air support from an unmanned aerial vehicle.

common, and specific component, in that order); and the final exercise dubbed FINEX.

Academic Phase

Students start the academics phase with generic lectures covering all the topics every student needs to know. More specifically to gain an understanding of functions that are outside of their respective field; electronic warfare and intelligence preparation of the battlefield being two examples.

Academics also provides an insight to all six functions of Marine aviation available to support the Marine Air-Ground Task Force (MAGTF): assault support, anti-aircraft warfare, offensive air support, electronic warfare, control of aircraft and missiles, and aerial reconnaissance.

Day one involves an inventory examination about topics that all students are expected to know. This gives

the instructors an initial snapshot of the level of preparation made by each student for the course.

Three days of academics follows, finishing with another test. Subjects include tactical risk management; teaching students to be risk managers and making them aware of the human factors that contribute to accidents. This crucial work involves the help of sports psychologists, physiologists, and athletes, all of whom address how to optimise performance and minimise distractions.

In any combat environment, an individual will be fatigued and stressed: both conditions contribute to degraded decision making. Stress on the students is constant during the course which affects their performance. While a degree of stress is considered important for performing at the highest level, lethargy does not necessarily lead to high quality performance. Consequently, each student must try to manage and departmentalise

Academics
Administration
Aviation C3
Aviation ground support
Aviation logistics
Aviation tactics development and evaluation
Command
Intelligence
Operations and training
Rotary wing
• Medium assault MV-22 division
• Heavy assault CH-53 division
• Utility UH-1Y division
• Attack AH-1Z division
Safety
Tactical aircraft (TACAIR)
• F-35 division
• Fighter attack F/A-18 division
• Forward air control airborne, tactical air control and reconnaissance division
• Light attack AV-8B division
• Transport KC-130 division
• Unmanned aerial systems RQ-7, RQ-21, and MQ-9 division

Right: **US Marines assigned to Combat Logistics Battalion 11 carry a TRV-150 unmanned aircraft system in preparation for a tactical resupply demonstration as part of WTI 2-23.** US Marine Corps/LCpl Ruben Padilla

In the third and fourth weeks of flight operations, the course enters the generic component which involves all types operating together as a MAGTF. An infantry battalion comprising about 1,000 marines providing the ground element participates in the generic component to add realism to the course. One example is an air assault involving the insertion of hundreds of marines into an objective area.

Despite the number of aircraft and helicopters deployed to Yuma for a WTI course, full replication of a real combat mission often requires participation of more aircraft. To bridge any gap, MAWTS-1 can either use live virtual construct training to simulate additional assets or request additional participants from the US Navy, US Air Force, and US Army.

Two examples in WTI 1-23 were the participation by US Army AH-64 Apache gunships, and a Royal Air Force Chinook. AH-64E Apache gunships participated in missions involving close air support training at Yodaville, Arizona and using a forward arming and refuelling point at a landing zone on the Chocolate Mountain Gunnery Range, California.

The Royal Air Force Chinook participated in a mission known as Assault Support Tactics 1 (AST-1), at Laguna Army Airfield, Arizona. AST-1 is a daytime, force-on-force event which affords the prospective Weapons and Tactics Instructors the opportunity to plan, brief, and execute a company-reinforced air assault while integrating the six functions of marine aviation.

In the more recent WTI 2-23, US Navy MH-60S Seahawk multi-mission helicopters participated in an assault support tactics mission.

The force-on force component, involving a living, breathing, and thinking enemy, offered by MAWTS-1 is deemed as the pinnacle of the training during the generic component. When students are presented with a passive or simulated enemy they learn a few lessons, but with no man in the loop, it's difficult to test tactics and how they would work in a real combat situation.

TACAIR aircraft fly to the Nellis Test and Training Range to use the robust threat array available there, while the ground forces operate in objective areas in ranges closer to Yuma.

When an infantry battalion was inserted into an objective area by MV-22s it was presented with cyber, electronic warfare, air-to-air and surface-to-air threats though there was no opposition manoeuvre force involved.

Yuma-based Marine Fighter Training Squadron 401 (VMFT-401) 'Snipers', a dedicated adversary unit equipped with F-5N Tiger IIs regularly provide the air-to-air threats and marines

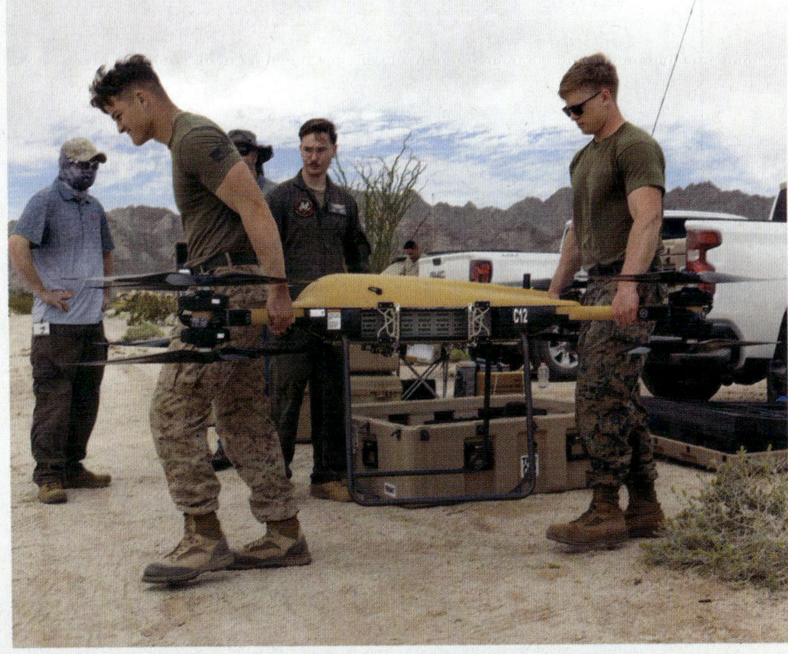

Below: **A TRV-150 unmanned aircraft system prepares to release a payload during a tactical resupply demonstration as part of WTI 2-23.** US Marine Corps/LCpl Ruben Padilla

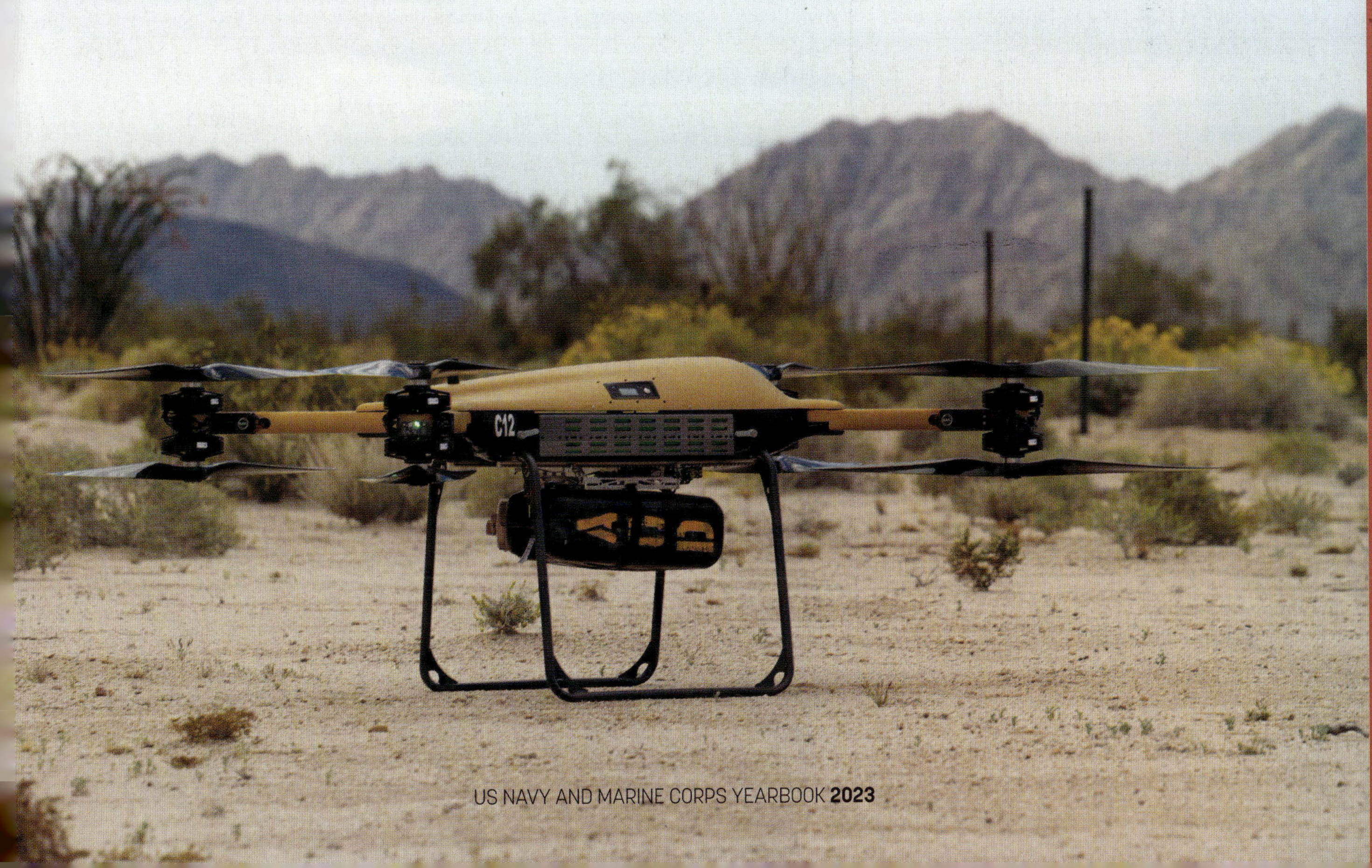

based at the range provide the surface-to-air threats.

In some missions, the ground force uses live ammunition. An air assault is a good example in which MV-22s airlift marines and CH-53s lift artillery systems, while AH-1Z Cobras, UH-1Y Hueys, AV-8B Harriers, F-35B Lightning IIs, and F/A-18 Hornets provide fire support to suppress the landing zone in advance of the troop insertion.

A notional enemy armed with artillery located close to the objective area would pose a direct threat to the marine battalion, which requires the battalion commanders to decide whether to defend their position or get back on the aircraft. If they opt to withdraw, the WTI students must decide how they execute that. This is a realistic scenario which gives an idea of the complexity of a combat engagement.

Final Exercise

The final phase of the WTI course is known as the final exercise, dubbed FINEX, and comprises three events (FINEX 1, FINEX 2 and FINEX 3) each involving one day of flying.

On day one of the final week (Monday), all students are presented with a scenario and a problem statement. Their task is to determine how to conduct the FINEX 1 mission the following day (Tuesday).

An intelligence update is issued on day three (Wednesday) showing how the enemy has responded and what the new threat is. This requires the students to look at different objective areas for the FINEX 2 mission on day four (Thursday) which usually requires all six functions of marine aviation to efficiently address the target set.

FINEX 2 includes a typical marine special operations forces (MARSOC) mission: a simulated casualty evacuation and a scenario involving the rescue of a downed pilot in the objective area.

Then on the final day of flying (Saturday) everything comes together in FINEX 3 which is the culmination of all previous phases. This so-called capstone event involves an air strike on targets located deep inside enemy territory and a follow-on air assault raid.

Surprises are introduced to the event, requiring the students to flex their original plan to an alternate. An example might involve pilots flying TACAIR jets who took off expecting to conduct close air support having to flex to provide direct air support.

FINEX 3 is the most challenging day of the course and occurs when the students are very tired, which requires the MAWTS-1 staff to account for the cumulative fatigue being experienced by the students, which is deemed to be similar to real combat, which impacts on their decision-making ability.

Strikes on the Nellis Test and Training Range and maritime strikes on the ranges over the Pacific to the west of San Diego are part of the three FINEX missions.

For each one, the students are presented with a robust peer level problem that they need to solve not only with the various US Marine Corps assets assembled at Marine Corps Air Station Yuma, but also other assets from the US Air Force and US Navy.

Graduation

Colonel Purcell and his staff have less than 24 hours to tally up each student's final course grade from the time the last aircraft lands during the Saturday evening to the graduation ceremony held at 16:00hrs on the Sunday. Before the graduation ceremony can get underway, on the Sunday morning all students attend a debrief for FINEX 3 to capture the lessons learnt from the last day of flying.

Student evaluation is updated every day of the course, so Col Purcell knows exactly how each student is doing when FINEX 3 starts. In a few cases, students don't succeed at WTI which the MAWTS-1

Above: **A TRV-150 unmanned aircraft system transports a box of Meals Ready-to-Eat during a tactical resupply demonstration as part of WTI 2-23.** US Marine Corps/LCpl Ruben Padilla

staff deem to be correlated between a student's level of preparation and performance.

The clock continues to tick after the graduation ceremony with the assembled group of aircraft and the new WTIs needed at their respective units. Within a few days of graduation some of the new WTIs will be deployed on ships and others at locations where combat operations are ongoing.

Other Aspects

MAWTS-1 is also tasked with developing tactics for Marine aviation, a role conducted by the squadron's Aviation Development, Tactics and Evaluation (ADT&E) department which is not part of the US Navy and US Marine Corps' operational test community.

Technology and innovation form a big part of the ADT&E department's work; each WTI course enables MAWTS-1 to conduct tactical demonstrations of new equipment.

Generally, there are two classifications of technologies that MAWTS-1 can evaluate during a course – those being considered by the Department of Defense and those that are already a Program of Record and will enter service with the fleet in the future.

Introducing New Capabilities

When the course needs to accommodate new capabilities provided by a new type like the CH-53K, collaboration between the MAWTS-1 staff and the aviation department, Headquarters US Marine Corps, is key.

The CH-53K has a team that is responsible for managing the programme. In conjunction with the Marine Corps Development Command based at Quantico, Virginia, the team develops concepts of employment for all aircraft, in case this the CH-53K.

The CH-53K programme team provides MAWTS-1 with the US Marine Corps' concept of employment for the aircraft. In addition, MAWTS-1 works with the test community based at Naval Air Station Patuxent River, Maryland and Naval Air Weapons Station China Lake, California, and Marine Operational Test and Evaluation Squadron 1 (VMX-1) based at Yuma to get early insight of the aircraft and its capabilities.

By understanding the CH-53K, its capabilities and its concept of employment, the MAWTS-1 instructors will be able to create a syllabus to optimise the capability of the heavy-lift helicopter and when it's integrated with the other types in the Aviation Combat Element.

Constant changes in operating environments, technology and weapons deem it necessary for instructors and staff working in all the different aircraft divisions at MAWTS-1 to continuously re-write standard operating procedures. For the marines involved, it's an exciting aspect of MAWTS-1 given the squadron's position within the Department of Defense and being on the leading edge of determining how the US Marine Corps will fight with the new types.

In addition to its training objectives, the WTI course is deemed as a large combat experiment. MAWTS-1 performs a mission in the way that's deemed sensible, against a realistic threat array akin to the real world, and measures the notional losses sustained during the missions. If an aircraft is notionally lost to a man-portable air defence system, a determination of what may have caused the loss is made during the mission debrief. Were the tactics executed correctly? Were the wrong tactics used? The process happens continuously throughout the course.

After each course, the MAWTS-1 staff holds what's known as a 'hot wash', which is

Below: A KC-46A Pegasus tanker aircraft assigned to New Hampshire Air National Guard's 157th Aerial Refueling Wing, refuels MV-22B Osprey tiltrotor aircraft en route to an airfield in the Utah Test and Training Range during a Marine Expeditionary Unit exercise for WTI 2-23. US Marine Corps/ LCpl Alejandro Fernandez

Right: **AH-1Z Vipers prepare to take-off at Marine Corps Air Station Yuma, Arizona, loaded with AGM-179 Joint Air-to-Ground Missiles for a test firing during WTI 2-23. US Marine Corps/LCpl Amelia Kang**

Below: **US Marine all airborne and air delivery specialists assigned to the 1st Landing Support Battalion, 1st Marine Logistics Group, exit a KC-130J Hercules aircraft during static line airborne operations near Yuma as part of WTI 2-23. US Marine Corps/LCpl Ruben Padilla**

deemed to be one of the most important weeks' worth of work of the year.

The staff look at every event completed in the course and the critiques provided by the students from every class on the course. By combing the two sets of data, and being tough on themselves, the staff address the tough questions posed by the analysis. Why did a mission fall short in one area or not achieve mission success? What needs to be done to make it better next time?

Each subsequent course is subtly different to the previous edition because of this exacting process, although the syllabus looks very similar. A balance must be struck between implementing subtle differences to the course while still achieving all the requirements.

Consideration is given to the impact of removing specific events, and whether that decision makes the course tactically unsound for a follow-on mission requirement.

The MAWTS-1 staff must also avoid the potential for surprises to be faced by WTIs in a real-world situation, simply because something was missed on the course.

Similar processes are also undertaken for all new munitions and weapons.

During 21 days of flight operations for WTI 2-23, aircraft assigned to MAWTS-1 dropped nearly 75,000lb of ordnance which included every weapon in the inventory. Statistics are recorded for the performance of every single weapon dropped including the effect on target.

Operations analysts assess the statistics, course by course, year by year, to determine if performance during the live course has improved. All data is submitted to the department responsible for ordnance.

Each WTI course yields an extensive evaluation of the weapons dropped and each weapon type's suitability for strike requirements by fleet pilots. The accumulated weapons data is used by MAGTF commanders to guide them in choosing which weapons to use in combat.

Commenting, Col Purcell said: "We try to make sure we are forward looking as much as possible when it comes to a new weapon, so we can determine how to employ it before it arrives in the fleet."

An example is the Navy Marine Expeditionary Ship Interdiction System dubbed NMESIS which carries two

Left: US Marines assigned to Marine Unmanned Aerial Vehicle Squadron 2 (VMU-2) recover an RQ-21A Blackjack aircraft at the Canon Air Defense Complex near Yuma, Arizona, during WTI 1-23. US Marine Corps/LCpl Ruben Padilla

Left: US Marines assigned to Marine Unmanned Aerial Vehicle Squadron 2 (VMU-2) prepare an RQ-21A Blackjack for launch during WTI 1 23 at the Canon Air Defense Complex near Yuma, Arizona. US Marine Corps/LCpl Ruben Padilla

Left: A CH-53K King Stallion helicopter assigned to Marine Heavy Helicopter Squadron 461 (HMH-461) conducts an external lift of two High Mobility Multipurpose Wheeled Vehicles during WTI 2-23 at an auxiliary airfield near Yuma, Arizona. US Marine Corps/ LCpl Ricardo Ramirez

Above: **An AH-1Z Viper attack helicopter conducts close air support exercise, during WTI 2-23.** US Marine Corps/LCpl Alejandro Fernandez

Naval Strike Missile containers on a remotely-operated unmanned Joint Light Tactical Vehicle.

Col Purcell said: "The fleet doesn't have representative models of NMESIS yet, but we know how the missile fires, flies, and what its capabilities are. In the future, when the first NMESIS missiles are fired during the course, the event might be considered to be the first time we've dealt with the NMESIS missile, but theoretically, we've already been working with it for the past year."

Amphibious Warfare

To support the Marine Corps' amphibious warfare capability during the desert-locked training undertaken for the WTI course, MAWTS-1 has a scenario that overlays the entire course. A large area of land is designated as an ocean, to notionally incorporate naval warfare into course scenarios.

A naval component also participates in the course MEUEX (Marine Expeditionary Unit exercise) which involves staging long-range raids by AV-8Bs, F-35Bs and MV-22s launched from simulated ships under the command of the C3 division.

A US Navy Tactical Air Control Squadron based in San Diego deploys to Yuma to provide a quality assurance check on how a raid is launched from a landing strip which looks like an amphibious assault ship, located out in the field.

Aviation Ground Support

Aviation ground support teaches three courses simultaneously throughout the WTI period of instruction: the primary aviation ground support course, one for marine survey and assault zone assessment (MSAZA) and one for forward aviation refuelling point officer in charge (FARP OIC). Each teaches the engineering and surveying skills required to support aviation operations with smaller equipment and manpower requirements. This designed to increase the team's ability to move throughout different areas of operation.

The MSAZA course, developed in partnership with the US Air Force, teaches marines the ability to survey a runway, a landing zone, or a drop zone in a manner common to the joint force.

The FARP OIC course teaches marines to understand all things involved with marine aviation, and how to run a forward aviation refuelling point.

Questions

Colonel Purcell poses two questions to all students at the start of their course. What is a WTI? and What is the WTI course?

Explaining his reasoning for those two questions, Col Purcell said: "I tell students a WTI is two things that enable five abilities. First and foremost, a WTI will become a subject matter expert in everything dealing with their individual type-model-series platform. That level of expertise combined with the missions and events encountered on the course, should make them an integrator and a mission planner for the MAGTF.

The two roles essentially enable five other abilities.

"Their expertise in their type-model-series platform makes them a training officer who can instruct on that type and a leader, whether it's a flight leader in the aircraft or a leader on the ground side. They go back to the fleet, and are required to train up all the officers, whether they are engineers serving with the AGS unit or pilots serving with a squadron to meet their mission. They are also the primary advisor to their commanding officer in terms of the readiness of the squadron and its pilots.

"We also instruct our students on risk management with respect to both the red and the blue threats, and how to make the right risk-informed decisions about how to get the mission done, which involves accounting for what the enemy can do to us and what we can do to ourselves if we don't consider all of the contributing factors that can increase the risk on a mission.

Summing up, Colonel Purcell said: "The WTI course is an in depth seven-week event that exposes all students to everything they need to plan and fight missions, across the full range of military operations, be it in an uncertain environment in a non-combatant evacuation operation, an air policing no fly zone role, through to the high-end fight against peer threats in GPS and communication-denied environments."

Right: **A member of a Tactical Air Control Party uses a common laser range finder during a close air support exercise at Wiss Airfield, California, during WTI 2-23. US Marine Corps/LCpl Alejandro Fernandez**

READY, RELEVANT
AND CAPABLE

An overview of the 26th Marine Expeditionary Unit's
pre-deployment training programme.

THE 26TH MARINE Expeditionary Unit (MEU) is a rapid response force capable of conducting amphibious operations, crisis response, and limited contingency operations. Currently embarked onboard the USS *Bataan* (LHD-5), the 26th MEU undertook its pre-deployment training program (PTP) in December 2022.

A MEU starts its seven-month pre-deployment training program (PTP) by completing a MAGTF Interoperability Course (a combination of raids, intelligence, TRAP and MSPF interoperability operations) which provides an opportunity to integrate multiple elements within the MEU to complete various scenario-based tasks and missions.

An Expeditionary Operations Training Group (EOTG), an organisation assigned to the Marine Expeditionary Force, provides an assessment of essential objectives. These include integrating individual and small unit skills, refining command and control procedures, and refining standard operating procedures prior to deployment.

Scenario-based events include company (reinforced) raids, Tactical Recovery of Aircraft Personnel (TRAP), Maritime Special Purpose Force (MSPF) missions, and intelligence gathering and planning. These training events are developed to give the MEU commander the maximum amount of flexibility in employment of forces and demonstrate the MEU's capability to integrate the MSPF with other sections to complete scenario-based missions.

MSPF is the premiere reconnaissance and collections force which enhances the MEU commander's awareness of the battle space with the support of other sections.

Below: **A sailor assigned to USS *Bataan* (LHD 5) stands watch as the amphibious assault ship transits the Suez Canal with the 26th Marine Expeditionary Unit on August 6, 2023.** US Marine Corps/ Cpl Nayelly Nieves-Nieves

Left: An MV-22B Osprey, attached to Marine Medium Tiltrotor Squadron 162 (Reinforced), lifts off during a unit level training exercise in Djibouti on August 8, 2023. While in Djibouti the 26th MEU Aviation Combat Element conducted reduced visibility landings. US Marine Corps/ Sgt Matthew Romonoyske-Bean

MEUEX I

The MAGTF Interoperability Course transitions directly into Marine Expeditionary Unit Exercise I (MEUEX I) designed to hone the MEU's warfighting skills and strengthen its core crisis response capabilities.

MEUEX I, a 15-day field exercise, is the first of several collective MAGTF training events associated with the MEU's Pre-deployment Training Programme (PTP). The PTP trains and evaluates an MEU preparing to deploy and is designed to build confidence and capabilities through increasingly more complex situations and environments.

The objective of MEUEX I is to focus on building unit cohesion while planning and executing land-based MEU missions across the full mission set within a realistic threat-based scenario building upon the lessons learned during the MAGTF Interoperability Course.

MEUEX I demonstrates the flexibility and operational reach of a land-based MEU by conducting long-range aviation strikes, night raids, Foreign Humanitarian Assistance (FHA) missions, Focused Collection Operations (FCO), embassy reinforcement and a Non-combatant Evacuation Operation (NEO), and contingency operations like Tactical Recovery of Aircraft and Personnel (TRAP), Quick Reaction Force (QRF), and casualty evacuation (CASEVAC) – typical missions that a MEU MAGTF may be tasked by the geographic combatant commander to support while forward deployed.

In the case of the 26th MEU, MEUEX I, held in early January 2023, tested its ability to provide sustained combat support while simultaneously enhancing its interoperability with the MEU through scenarios rehearsing core tasks such as providing an evacuation control centre in support of NEO and FHA operations.

Deployed alongside the USS *Bataan* Amphibious Ready Group (ARG), the 26th MEU provides a forward-deployed, flexible, MAGTF capable of conducting amphibious operations, crisis response, and limited contingency operations, to include enabling of follow-on forces and designated special operations, in support of the geographic combatant commander's theatre requirements.

The *Bataan* ARG includes the amphibious assault ship USS *Bataan* (LHD 5), the amphibious transport ship USS *Mesa Verde* (LPD 19), and the amphibious dock landing ship USS *Carter Hall* (LSD 50).

Below: A US Marine Corps AV-8B Harrier II aircraft, attached to Marine Medium Tiltrotor Squadron 162, 26th Marine Expeditionary Unit (MEU), in the Gulf of Oman, on Aug. 14, 2023. US Marine Corps/ Sgt Matthew Romonoyske-Bean

Right: **An MV-22 Osprey assigned to the 26th Marine Expeditionary Unit (Special Operations Capable) lands on a hilltop during flight operations from Bardufoss, Norway, Aug. 7, 2023.** US Marine Corps/Cpl Aziza Kamuhanda

Below: **Amphibious assault ship USS *Bataan* (LHD 5) transits through the Red Sea on August 8, 2023.** US Navy/Mass Communication Specialist Riley Gasdia

In late January 2023, marines and sailors assigned to the 26th MEU completed a Visit, Board, Search and Seizure (VBSS) event designed to simulate conducting a real-world maritime interception operation, one that may arise during the 26th MEU's upcoming deployment to 5th and 6th Fleet areas of operation. US Navy and US Marine Corps personnel conduct non-simulated VBSS operations to combat terrorism, piracy, and smuggling. A VBSS operation can also be used to capture enemy vessels and to undertake inspections, such as customs and safety, to enforce international law and ensure that a vessel is seaworthy.

Deemed as an advanced course, MEUEX I is evaluated by the Special Tactics Branch of the Expeditionary Operations Training Group, in terms of training and evaluating personnel assigned to the MEU in their ability to execute key MAGTF Mission Essential Tasks (METs) to conduct maritime interception operations.

The MEUEX I integrated the MSPF, Battalion Landing Team 1/6, Marine Medium Tiltrotor Squadron 162

(VMM-162), Combat Logistics Battalion 22 (CLB), and personnel from explosive ordnance disposal, counter-intelligence/human intelligence, and the Bataan ARG. Integrating these units into a cohesive force is critical for mission success conducted while deployed.

PHIBRON-MEU Integration

During the follow-on PHIBRON MEU Integration Training or PMINT, 26th MEU marines conducted a VBSS using 35ft rigid inflatable boats or RIBS, to locate, board, search, and seize a simulated enemy vessel. PHIBRON is the abbreviation for an Amphibious Squadron, a tactical and administrative organisation comprising amphibious assault ships used to transport marines and their equipment for an amphibious assault operation.

During PMINT, the 26th MEU loaded a HIMARS rocket system onto a landing craft for transportation from a beachhead at Marine Corps Base Camp Lejeune to the USS *Mesa Verde* (LPD 19) off the coast of North Carolina. It was the first such loading conducted on the east coast. A HIMARS utilises guided-missiles and rockets fired to a range of 84km. The mobility of the HIMARS launcher allows it to operate in disparate environments, insert rapidly via surface or air, and provide significant firepower to a ground force.

Cpl Luke Tarvin, a HIMARS section chief assigned to 1st Platoon, Sierra Battery said: "The HIMARS capability provides the 26th MEU a lethal force that can shoot far, be mobile and communicate across the MAGTF."

During PMINT, the 26th MEU successfully accomplished all its training objectives including rapidly embarking the MAGTF via air and surface assets, conducting carrier qualifications/deck landing qualifications, refining standard operating procedures, and conducting typical MEU amphibious operations such as Defence of the Amphibious Task Force (DATF) during transits within restricted waterways, air assaults, and limited scale raids.

Below:
Amphibious assault ship USS *Bataan* (LHD 5) and Dock landing ship USS *Carter Hall* (LSD 50) transit in formation through the Red Sea on August 8, 2023.
US Navy/Mass Communication Specialist Riley Gasdia

Left: **Marines assigned to the 26th MEU (SOC), perform maintenance on the brake connectors of a MV-22B Osprey, attached to Marine Medium Tilt Rotor Squadron 162 (reinforced), aboard the USS** *Bataan* **(LHD 5).** US Navy/Mass Communication Specialist Riley Gasdia

MEUEX II

The PMINT exercise culminated with an opportunity to train to the initial stages of an amphibious assault intended to seize key maritime terrain with the full debarkation of the MEU MAGTF. This culmination event marked the transition from PMINT's sea-based operation to MEUEX II - a three-day land-based training exercise focussed on a fire support control and a live-fire raid by a motorised infantry company.

The team was able to build proficiency in ship-to-shore movements, accomplish initial deck landing qualifications for several pilots and aircrew, achieve C5I (Command, Control, Communication, Computer, Cyber and Intelligence) capabilities while demonstrating competency in the ability to command and control an operation from the sea, and demonstrated proficiency in the rapid response planning process.

In accordance with Force Design 2030 modernisation initiatives, PMINT provided the 26th MEU with an opportunity to integrate the Light Marine Air Defence Integrated System or L-MADIS, a capability to deter and neutralise unmanned aircraft systems. L-MADIS can be employed expeditiously on ship or on land to protect high value assets.

Commander Chuck Cha, *Bataan* ARG information warfare commander said: "During PMINT, the *Bataan* ARG/26th MEU showcased high-end information warfare integration. The team demonstrated the ability to implement the appropriate command and control structure to execute integrated non-kinetic fires capabilities across the force. This was achieved by combining electronic warfare capabilities in support of DATF missions."

Below: **A Utility Task Vehicle disembarks a US Navy landing craft during an amphibious assault on Onslow Beach, North Carolina, on June 2, 2023. The assault was the final event of Composite Training Unit Exercise (C2X) providing training of marine movement from ship to shore.** US Marine Corps/ Cpl Tyler Raab

MEUEX III

For two weeks in March 2023, personnel with the 26th MEU successfully completed their final land-based exercise, MEUEX III, which involved conducting distributed operations within the littorals of eastern Virginia, North Carolina, South Carolina, Georgia, and Louisiana. This as part of the unit's PTP was designed to ensure the 26th MEU had the battle staff competencies and operational capabilities required to function as a forward-deployed expeditionary crisis response force.

During MEUEX III, the 26th MEU successfully achieved C5ISR capabilities and demonstrated proficiency in all MEU Mission Essential Tasks (METs) including land-based distributed operations within the littorals of the eastern shoreline, an airfield seizure, long-range raids, long-range expeditionary strikes, focused intelligence collection, company-level live fire training, littoral operations, Special Insertion and Extraction (SPIE) and a day/night Fire Support Coordination exercise (FSCEX).

Captain Vernon Atkinson, firepower control team leader, 26th MEU said: "The FSCEX phase of MEUEX III focused on integrating surface and air-delivered fires within a defined battlespace – to include a live-fire HIMARS mission via long-haul digital communication. The exercise construct showcased the ability of the MEU Fires and Effects Coordination Center (FECC) and battalion Fire Support Coordination Center (FSCC) to command-and-control multiple firing agencies to maximise effects on the battlefield in support of MAGTF manoeuvre. It proved a significant step forward regarding our MEU/SOF integration."

MEUEX III was the culminating land-based littoral exercise for the 26th MEU and set the conditions for the unit to transition with the Bataan ARG into the advanced stage of PTP for ARGMEUEX (AMX) followed by final certification during Composite Training Unit Exercise (COMPTUEX).

ARGMUEX

Over a five-day period during the ARGMUEX in late April 2023, a US consulate in the small, fictitious, country of Obsidian was surrounded by protestors upset with the American presence in their coastal nation within the Treasure Coast region. Violence increased and the regional situation continued to deteriorate.

In response to the situation, the 26th MEU conducted several missions.

First, its Forward Command Element (FCE) was deployed to liaise with Department of State and other representatives at the consulate. An FCE is a unique MEU capability specially trained to rapidly deploy to integrate

Right: **A landing craft assigned to Assault Craft Unit 4, transits toward the well deck of the amphibious dock landing ship USS *Carter Hall* (LSD 50) during the *Bataan* ARG's COMPTUEX, the final pre-deployment exercise that certifies the *Bataan* ARG and 26th MEU's ability to conduct military operations.**
US Navy/Mass Communication Specialist Moises Sandoval

Below: **US Marines assigned to the 26th Marine Expeditionary Unit conduct an amphibious assault raid during COMPTUEX at Marine Corps Base Camp Lejeune, North Carolina, on June 2, 2023.**
US Marine Corps/ Cpl Kyle Jia

with representatives from across the interagency, partners and allies to set conditions for follow-on MEU MAGTF operations or activities.

Once the FCE arrived, it planned and coordinated MEU resources to support contingency response options for the Department of State.

This NEO training scenario began with the rapid insertion of a specialised security force to protect and defend the consulate/embassy, and then escalated into a full NEO where American citizens were evacuated and transported to the ships of the *Bataan* ARG and follow-on safe havens.

The NEO training provided an opportunity to work through the steps in the process, and to refine standard operating procedures. In this scenario, that meant positioning ships in the right area to ensure the Marines could respond quickly, to realistic interactions with members from the Department of State, to conduct riot control and respond to realistic contingencies, to setting up the

Evacuation Control Center (ECC), and to conduct the evacuation and processing of evacuees aboard ships in support of national interests and national security objectives within the region: a unique capability held by the navy and Marine Corps team.

NEOs are a critical Marine Essential Task special to MEUs that involve the rapid deployment of personnel to support a disaggregated location – normally meaning the use of aircraft from aboard ship to shore, and back aboard – the positioning of ships to best support the transportation of people, medical capabilities ranging from basic screening to potential life-saving care, and finally the communications network to ensure everything flows smoothly.

By the end of the five-day event, the *Bataan* ARG and 26th MEU had successfully evacuated over 500 Americans and consular personnel to a staging location and subsequently flew them to the USS *Bataan* (LHD 5), USS *Mesa Verde* (LPD 19), and the USS

Carter Hall (LSD 50) operating in the Atlantic Ocean.

On May 1, 2023, a small task-organised element of the 26th MEU deployed on short notice to the US Central Command (CENTCOM) area of operations. The deployment started during the final stage of its PTP which demonstrated the 26th MEU's credentials as a crisis response force and tested its ability to aggregate forces at a moment's notice to support operations across the globe.

The ARGMEUEX (AMX) was the sixth of seven large scale pre-deployment events within the 26th MEU's PTP that ensured the MEU is properly task-organised and capable of executing all MEU MAGTF METs prior to COMPTUEX.

AMX provided an opportunity for the 26th MEU to replicate MAGTF operations on-land and from-the-sea including Maritime Interdiction Operations (MIO), Defence of the Amphibious Task Force (DATF), Expeditionary Advanced Based Operations (EABO), VBSS, multiple live-fire raids, information operations

TODAY

Airforces Monthly is devoted entirely to modern military aircraft and their air arms.

shop.keypublishing.com/afmsubs

Combat Aircraft Journal is renowned for being America's best-selling military aviation magazine.

shop.keypublishing.com/casubs

ing.com

(IO), strikes, long-range reconnaissance, focused collection operations and operational preparation of the environment, an embassy/consulate reinforcement with a security force (SECFOR), to the rapid deployment of the 26th MEU FCE to liaise with Department of State representatives, a NEO, and culminating with a dynamic amphibious assault to seize key terrain in preparation for follow-on operations associated with the scenario.

The 26th MEU also demonstrated the ability to conduct rapid planning and contingency operations by serving as the TARP force and standing missions requiring a QRF to support other forces within the scenario.

The exercise provided another opportunity for the 26th MEU to codify common tactics, techniques, and procedures (TTPs) and standard operating procedures (SOP) with the *Bataan* ARG and SOF elements supporting the exercise.

Elements of the 26th MEU's MSPF completed an advanced MEU/SOF integrated raid course during the first week of AMX, enhancing and serving as a culminating event to finalise MEU/SOF TTPs and SOPs.

Colonel Dennis Sampson, commanding officer of the 26th MEU (SOC) said: "AMX provided the 26th MEU with a great opportunity to showcase the relevance, flexibility, and all-domain operational capability the ARG/MEU team provides a geographic combatant commander, fleet commander, or joint special operations task force commander. AMX also highlighted the importance of having a forward-deployed MEU, embarked aboard US Navy amphibious ships. The MEU MAGTF, when combined with the *Bataan* ARG, is the nation's premier crisis response force capable of responding across the full spectrum of military operations and capable of exploiting the asymmetric advantages the sea provides as manoeuvre space over our potential adversaries."

During AMX, the navy-marine corps team successfully completed their first integrated live-fire exercise (ILFE), which demonstrated the firepower and flexible response options the ARG/MEU team has for offensive and defensive operations within the littorals. Lieutenant Commander Jesse Packard, operations officer, PHIBRON 8 said: "The live-fire event demonstrates the team's ability to defend the amphibious task force and engage the adversary using combined arms fires. During ILFE, the *Bataan* ARG/26th MEU

Right: **Elements of the 26th Marine Expeditionary Unit executed a simulated airfield seizure from the ships of the *Bataan* ARG and established a Forward Arming and Refuelling Point during COMPTUEX.** US Marine Corps/Cpl Aziza Kamuhanda

Below: **US Marines prepare to load low-drag general purpose bombs onto an AV-8B Harrier, assigned to VMM-162, on the flight deck of amphibious assault ship USS *Bataan* (LHD 5) during COMPTUEX.** US Navy/Mass Communication Specialist Darren Newell

Left: **A UH-1Y Venom takes off from the flight deck of the amphibious transport dock ship USS *Mesa Verde* (LPD 19) during COMPTUEX, the final pre-deployment exercise that certified the *Bataan* ARG and 26th MEU's ability to conduct military operations through joint planning and execute challenging and realistic scenarios.** US Navy/Ensign Kyle Clement

integrated all three ships, AH-1Zs, UH-1Ys and MH-60S helicopters and other ground elements of the 26th MEU. Moreover, the ship's force enhanced the capabilities of the *Bataan* ARG to defend themselves against an asymmetrical threat."

CBRN

In late May, chemical, biological, radiological, and nuclear (CBRN) defence specialists assigned to the 26th MEU completed a five-day CBRN hazard training course with Guardian Centers, a government contractor based in Perry, Georgia.

Training provided to the 26th MEU specialists included wide area searches, radiation dose mapping, sampling, site characterisation and mission profile events in a realistic environment. The training took place at the Guardian Center town which is designed to train military and civilians in disaster response bombings and CBRN related events.

A CBRN team is attached to every major subordinate command in the US Marine Corps, including the 26th MEU. The team is responsible for conducting CBRN defence monitoring, providing chemical detection, gathering biological agent collection, and sampling, and executing protective measures and first aid to unit personnel.

Above: **Marines assigned to the 26th MEU transport live Joint Air-to-Ground missiles on the flight deck of USS *Bataan* (LHD 5).** US Navy/Mass Communication Specialist Riley Gasdia

Left: **Sailors chock and chain a CH-53E Sea Stallion helicopter to the flight deck aboard the amphibious dock landing ship USS *Carter Hall* (LSD 50) during COMPTUEX.** US Navy/Mass Communication Specialist Moises Sandoval

Instructor-led academics, where the CBRN specialists practiced detecting hazardous materials, conducting chemical sampling and the reading of those samples, started the course.

Training culminated with an event in which marines wore hazardous material protective clothing and equipment used to scan for radiation, recover and decontaminate a casualty.

The training provides the 26th MEU with a capability to respond to and remove a chemical or biological threat such as weapon of mass destruction, spills or fires involving hazardous materials, as well as accidents involving such hazardous materials.

Trident 23-4

Between May 18-22, 2023, the 26th MEU's Maritime Special Purpose Force (MSPF) integrated with Naval Special Warfare Operators or SEALs during Exercise Trident 23-4. The two units conducted direct-action SOF raid training and advanced training focused on Military Assisted Departure (MAD) and Non-combatant Evacuation Operations (NEO).

Elements assigned to the 26th MEU that participated in the exercise included MV-22 Osprey tilt-rotors from the 26th MEU ACE, the 26th MEU MSPF,

and several planners from the 26th MEU Command Element during the early stages of COMPTUEX (C2X) - the MEU's final at-sea, pre-deployment training exercise.

During one event, the 26th MEU MSPF served as the airborne Immediate Response Force (IRF) in a complex direct-action SOF raid within a threat-based scenario, one that was reflective of the US 5th and 6th Fleet areas of operation. An IRF is capable of quickly responding across the spectrum of contingencies that a raid force could encounter within the objective area during the mission.

COMPTUEX

Between May 16 and June 6, 2023, the *Bataan* ARG and the 26th MEU participated in COMPTUEX (C2X), the final deployment certification training event prior to deployment. The 26th MEU was deployed aboard the USS *Bataan* (LHD 5), the USS *Mesa Verde* (LPD 19), and the USS *Carter Hall* (LSD 50).

During COMPTUEX, elements of the 26th MEU conducted a simulated Foreign Humanitarian Assistance (FHA) mission at the Guardian Center in Perry, Georgia on May 24-27.

An FHA is a type of mission conducted to directly relieve or reduce human

Left: **A pair of KC-130J Hercules assigned to Special Purpose Marine Air-Ground Task Force Crisis Response in formation prior to performing night aerial refuelling with MV-22B Ospreys near the southern coast of Spain.** US Marine Corps/ Cpl Michael Petersheim

rapid expansion into a larger force as a situation demands by simply adding forces as needed to the core units of each existing element.

Core Elements

All MAGTFs consist of four core elements: a command element, a ground combat element (GCE), an aviation combat element (ACE), and a logistics combat element (LCE).

The **Command Element** is the MAGTF headquarters, which task-organises to provide the command-and-control capabilities required for effective planning, execution, and assessment of operations.

Additionally, the command element can exercise command and control within a joint force from the sea or ashore and act as a joint task force headquarters core element. The command element may include additional command and control and intelligence capabilities from national and theatre-based assets, force reconnaissance assets, signals intelligence capabilities from the radio battalion, and a force fires coordination centre. A command element can employ additional major subordinate commands, such as the force artillery headquarters, naval construction regiments, or US Army manoeuvre or engineering units.

The **Ground Combat Element** (GCE) task-organises to conduct ground operations in support of the MAGTF's mission. A GCE is usually formed around an infantry organisation reinforced with artillery, reconnaissance, light armoured reconnaissance, assault amphibian,

tank, and engineer forces. The GCE can vary in size and composition from a rifle platoon to one or more divisions. It is the only MAGTF element that can seize and occupy terrain.

The **Aviation Combat Element** (ACE) task-organises to conduct air operations, project combat power, and contribute to battlespace dominance in support of the MAGTF's mission by performing some or all six functions of US Marine Corps aviation: anti-air warfare, assault support, electronic warfare, offensive air support, air reconnaissance, and control of aircraft and missiles.

The ACE consists of an aviation headquarters with air control agencies,

aircraft squadrons or groups, and logistic units. It can vary in size and composition from a small aviation detachment of specifically required aircraft to one or more Marine Aircraft Wings.

An ACE may operate from ships or from austere expeditionary locations ashore and can transition between them without loss of capability. It exercises command and control throughout the battlespace.

The **Logistics Combat Element** (LCE) task-organises to provide all functions of tactical logistics necessary to support the continued readiness and sustainability of the MAGTF. The LCE performs some or all six functions of tactical logistics: supply,

Below: **An MV-22B Osprey assigned to Special-Purpose Marine Air-Ground Task Force Crisis Response from Marine Medium Tiltrotor Squadron 162 (VMM-162) prepares to aerial refuel with a KC-130J over the Mediterranean Sea.** US Marine Corps/SSgt Tanner Iskra

maintenance, transportation, health services, and general engineering. Others include legal, exchange, food, disbursing, postal, billeting, religious, mortuary, and morale and recreation services.

The LCE may vary in size and composition from a support detachment up to one or more logistic groups. The LCE operates from sea bases or from expeditionary bases established ashore and may be the main effort of the MAGTF during foreign humanitarian assistance missions or selected phases of maritime prepositioning operations.

The US Marine Corps operates five types of MAGTF:

Marine Expeditionary Forces or MEF
Marine Expeditionary Forces
  Forward or MEF(F)
Marine Expeditionary Brigades or MEB
Marine Expeditionary Units or MEU
Special Purpose Marine Airto-Ground
  Task Forces or SPMAGTF

Marine Expeditionary Forces

A Marine Expeditionary Force is the principal warfighting organisation of the US Marine Corps, each is capable of conducting and sustaining expeditionary operations in any geographic environment. Additionally, MEFs routinely task-organise subordinate units into smaller MAGTFs or other formations to support the geographic combatant commander's ongoing engagement and crisis response requirements.

The US Marine Corps operates three MEFs. Each one varies in size with the largest comprising approximately 40,000 marines and sailors.

As outline above, each MEF includes: a command element, a GCE of one Marine division (MARDIV), an ACE of one Marine Aircraft Wing (MAW), and an LCE from one Marine Logistics Group (MLG).

The three MEFs currently in operation are:

I MEF based in southern California and Arizona, under Commander, Marine Corps Forces Pacific with three major subordinate commands: the 1st Marine Division, 3d Marine Aircraft Wing, and the 1st Marine Logistics Group.
II MEF based in North and South Carolina, under Commander, Marine Corps Forces Command with three major subordinate commands: the 2nd Marine Division, 2nd Marine Aircraft Wing, and the 2nd Marine Logistics Group.
III MEF based in Okinawa, mainland Japan, Hawaii, and Guam, under Commander, Marine Corps Forces Pacific with three major subordinate commands: the 3rd Marine Division, 1st Marine Aircraft Wing, and the 3rd Marine Logistics Group.

A deployed MEF, in addition to its normally assigned units, may command units from other MEFs, the Marine Corps Forces Reserve, other services and nations, and

Left: **Marines assigned to Marine Unmanned Aerial Vehicle Squadron 1 (VMU-1) prepare to launch an RQ-21 Blackjack drone on the Yuma range in Arizona.** US Marine Corps/LCpl Rhita Daniel

US Special Operations Command. When augmented with forces from other MEFs, the deployed MEF can have multiple GCEs, such as I MEF during Operation Desert Storm, which had both the 1st and 2nd Marine Corps Divisions and a US Army armoured brigade.

Augmenting aviation units from other US Marine Corps sources normally operate within a single ACE. Additional US Marine Corps, US Navy, and US Army logistic units may augment an LCE, as happened during Operation Iraqi Freedom. MEFs have grown to more than 90,000 marines, sailors, and soldiers.

A MEF typically deploys with 60 days of sustainment, which can be extended through external support from other services or a host nation. The MEF commander and his staff can form the nucleus for a joint task force, combined task force, or functional component headquarters.

Additionally, a MEF(Forward) is normally the lead echelon of a MEF, or, for some contingencies, it can be a stand-alone MAGTF capable of sustained expeditionary operations. Generally, a MEF(F) is smaller than a MEF and larger than a Marine Expeditionary Brigade. For example, a MEF(F) commanded by a major general deployed on a rotational basis to execute combat operations in Operations Iraqi Freedom and Enduring Freedom. The GCE of the MEF(F) normally consists of a division or multiple regiments.

Marine Expeditionary Brigade

A Marine Expeditionary Brigade (MEB) is a mid-sized MAGTF that conducts major security cooperation operations, responds to larger crises or contingencies, or participates in major operations and campaigns-such as those in Afghanistan. An MEB provides the building blocks for forcible entry and other power projection operations, providing the landing forces for amphibious assault and the fly-in echelons that marry-up with equipment and supplies delivered by maritime prepositioning ships. Back in 1990, during Operation Desert Shield, for example, two MEBs deployed via amphibious ships while marines and sailors from two other MEBs were flown to Saudi Arabia to fall in on equipment and 30 days of supplies delivered via maritime prepositioning ships. Normally commanded by brigadier generals, an MEB comprises approximately 16,000 marines and sailors once their subordinate units are assigned. A MEB normally consists of:

A command element, which may include additional assets, such as command and control, reconnaissance, signals intelligence capabilities from the radio battalion, and engineering capabilities from the naval construction regiments.

Below: **An F/A-18C Hornet assigned to Marine Fighter Attack Squadron 115 (VMFA-115) makes an arrested landing at Marine Corps Air Ground Combat Center, Twentynine Palms, California during a large-scale, combined-arms training exercise.** US Marine Corps/SSgt Kowshon Ye

A GCE composed of an infantry regiment reinforced with artillery, reconnaissance, engineers, light armoured reconnaissance units, assault amphibian units, and other attachments as required.

An ACE composed of combat assault transport helicopter/tilt-rotor aircraft (CH-53 and MV-22), utility and attack helicopters (UH-1Y and AH-1Z), vertical/short take-off and landing fixed-wing attack aircraft (F-35B and/or AV-8B), fighter-attack aircraft (F/A-18 and F-35C), unmanned aircraft systems (MQ-9A and RQ-21), air refuellers/transport aircraft (KC-130), and requisite aviation logistic and command and control capabilities.

An LCE task-organised around a combat logistics regiment. This element normally has engineering; supply; services; transportation; medical; maintenance capabilities; and landing support for beach, port, and airfield delivery operations.

The MEB command elements maintain close coordination and conduct operational planning with key joint and service headquarters and can rapidly assume control of forces for missions across the range of military operations.

Like the larger MEFs, MEBs may take in units from other services or nations and grow beyond its notional size. MEBs are the smallest MAGTFs capable of performing all six functions of marine aviation, which can conduct the full range

Right: Marines assigned to Marine Unmanned Aerial Vehicle Squadron 1 (VMU-1) set up an RQ-21 Blackjack drone for launch at the Canon Air Defense Complex in Yuma, Arizona. US Marine Corps/ LCpl John Hall

Middle: An F/A-18D Hornet assigned to Marine All Weather Attack Squadron 224 seconds from plugging into the drogue extended from the pod of a Multi-Point Refuelling System fitted to a US Air Force KC-135 Stratotanker. US Air Force/TSgt Robert Harnden

Below: F/A-18C Hornets attached to Marine Fighter Attack Squadron 115 (VMFA-115) flying along the Bab al Mandeb transit between the Red Sea and the Gulf of Aden. US Navy

An ACE composed of a combat assault transport helicopter/tilt-rotor squadron (CH-53 and MV-22), utility and attack helicopters (UH-1Y and AH-1Z), vertical/short take-off and landing fixed-wing attack aircraft (F-35B or AV-8B), unmanned aircraft systems (RQ-21), shore-based air refuellers/transport aircraft (KC-130), and other detachments, as required.

An LCE task-organised around a MEU combat logistics battalion, consisting of engineering, supply, services, transportation, landing support, medical, and maintenance capabilities.

There are seven MEU command elements. Six of them are in a rotational cycle that provides continuous forward presence with two ARG/MEUs in key regions. The seventh is permanently forward-deployed in Japan under the command of United

of expeditionary operations, and may serve as the lead echelon of the MEF. The MEB command element can also serve as the nucleus of a joint or multinational task force headquarters.

Marine Expeditionary Unit

The Marine Expeditionary Units or MEUs, embarked aboard US Navy ships assigned to Amphibious Ready Groups (ARGs), form ARG/MEUs which provide a continuous, forward naval presence in key regions to conduct a range of tasks. These included steady-state security cooperation, military engagement, and deterrence, as well as immediate response to episodic crises and contingencies. The ARG/MEUs can also support major operations and campaigns in a variety of ways, such as enabling the introduction of other forces, acting as the lead echelon for expansion to a larger formation, or providing the geographic combatant commander an inherently mobile and flexible sea-based reserve. A colonel commands a MEU. When embarked aboard an ARG, which is commanded by a US Navy captain, a support relationship is normally established between them. A MEU normally consists of:

A command element that may include additional command and control or signals intelligence assets.

A GCE formed around an infantry battalion landing team reinforced with artillery, reconnaissance, engineers, light armoured reconnaissance units, assault amphibian units, and other attachments, as required.

Above: **Marines assigned to Marine Light Helicopter Attack Squadron 775 (HMLA-775) refuel a UH-1Y Venom at a Forward Arming and Refuelling Point, a temporary facility organised, equipped, and deployed to provide fuel and ammunition necessary for the employment of aviation manoeuvring units in combat, at Marine Corps Air Ground Combat Center, Twentynine Palms, California.** US Marine Corps/ Cpl Ryan Schmid

Right: **An AH-1Z Viper attack helicopter approaches the flight deck of Royal Australian Navy Canberra-class landing helicopter dock HMAS *Canberra* (L02) during Exercise RIMPAC, the world's largest international maritime exercise.** Royal Australian Navy/ Leading Seaman Matthew Lyall

States Pacific Command. The seven MEU command elements are:

11th MEU, 13th MEU, and 15th MEU, under commander, Marine Corps Forces Pacific, which rotationally deploy with subordinate elements provided from I MEF.

22nd MEU, 24th MEU, and 26th MEU, under commander, Marine Corps Forces Command, which rotationally deploy with subordinate elements provided from II MEF.

31st MEU, under commander, Marine Corps Forces Pacific, part of the forward-deployed naval force in the Pacific. It periodically cruises with subordinate elements provided from III MEF. These elements include units that are permanently assigned, and others temporarily provided to III MEF from the other MEFs through the unit deployment program, for example a Marine Fighter Attack Squadron deployed to Marine Corps Air Station Iwakuni, Japan.

The major subordinate elements are normally assigned to rotational MEU command elements several months prior to deployment to undergo, in concert with the ARG, an extensive training and certification process (see pages 50-65).

Above: An F-35B Lightning II aircraft assigned to Marine Medium Tiltrotor Squadron 262 (VMM-262) lands on the flight deck of amphibious assault carrier USS *Tripoli* (LHA 7) while underway in the US 7th Fleet area of operations. US Navy/Mass Communication Specialist Malcolm Kelley

Left: A UH-1Y Venom helicopter assigned to Marine Light Attack Helicopter Squadron 773 (HMLA-773) on the flight deck of the USS *Mesa Verde* (LPD-19) during cross deck international ship landing operations off the coast of Brazil in support of exercise UNITAS LXIII, on September 16, 2022. US Marine Corps/Major Jeremy Wheeler

They usually deploy for six to seven months, carrying enough supplies for the MEU to conduct operations ashore for 15 days, beyond which they are normally sustained through the integrated naval logistics system. The forward-deployed ARG/MEU has a shorter work-up and deployment cycle. While forward, ARG/MEUs frequently conduct multiple, simultaneous missions distributed over a wide geographic area.

In 2010, a single ARG/MEU concurrently conducted foreign humanitarian assistance operations in Pakistan with CH-46 and CH-53 helicopters, strike operations in Afghanistan with AV-8B Harriers, and counterpiracy operations in the Gulf of Aden with AH-1 Cobra, UH-1 Huey and MH-60S Seahawk helicopters.

On return from deployment, an ARG/MEU remains in a stand-by status for 30 to 60 days, during which time it is held ready for immediate redeployment in response to a crisis, as happened following the 2010 earthquake in Haiti.

Special Purpose MAGTF

A Special Purpose MAGTF OR SPMAGTF is formed when situations arise for which a MEU or other unit is either inappropriate or unavailable. An SPMAGTF may be of any size - but normally no larger than a MEU - with tailored capabilities required to accomplish a particular mission. It may be task-organised from nondeployed

US Marine Corps forces or formed on a contingency basis from a portion of a deployed MAGTF.

Regimental-level headquarters often assume the role as a SPMAGTF command element and may conduct training in anticipated mission skills prior to establishment.

A SPMAGTF may deploy using commercial shipping or aircraft, inter-theatre airlift, amphibious shipping, or organic US Marine Corps aviation.

SPMAGTFs have often conducted sea-based security cooperation activities, such as Southern Partnership Station and Africa Partnership Station.

Southern Partnership Station is a US Naval Forces Southern Command/4th Fleet mission comprised of a series of deployments focused on subject matter exchanges with partner nation militaries, medical teams, and security forces in the Caribbean, Central and South America.

Africa Partnership Station is a US Naval Forces Africa Command maritime security cooperation programme comprising engagement activities with international partners and governmental/non-governmental organisations to enhance African partner nations' self-sustaining capability to effectively maintain maritime security within their inland waterways, territorial waters, and exclusive economic zones.

Left: **A CH-53E Super Stallion assigned to Marine Heavy Helicopter Squadron 772 (HMH-772) lifts a M777 howitzer for a helicopter support team training event during an Integrated Training Exercise (ITX) at Marine Corps Air Ground Combat Center, Twentynine Palms, California. ITX provides opportunities to increase combat readiness and lethality; and exercise MAGTF command and control of battalions and squadrons.** US Marine Corps/Cpl Ryan Schmid

Middle: **Marines assigned to Combat Logistics Battalion 25, 4th Marine Logistics Group prepare to hook a M777 howitzer for a helicopter support team training event during an Integrated Training Exercise at Marine Corps Air Ground Combat Center Twentynine Palms, California.** US Marine Corps/Cpl Ryan Schmid

Left: **Marines with Oscar Battery, 5th Battalion, 14th Marine Regiment prepare to load a M777 howitzer during an Integrated Training Exercise at Marine Corps Air Ground Combat Center, Twentynine Palms, California.** US Marine Corps/Cpl Ryan Schmid

Other SPMAGTFs have been formed to provide sea-based foreign humanitarian assistance or military support to civil authorities or participate in freedom of navigation operations.

An important type of SPMAGTF is called an alert contingency MAGTF. Each of the three MEFs usually maintains an alert contingency MAGTF as an on-call, rapid crisis response force. A MEF commander may prescribe that an alert contingency MAGTF be ready to initiate deployment to any location worldwide within a certain number of days or hours, depending on the indications and warnings associated with an emerging crisis. Because of the rapid requirement to deploy so rapidly, readiness is paramount. Equipment and supplies intended for use as part of an alert contingency MAGTF are identified and, where appropriate, staged for immediate embarkation. The alert contingency MAGTF usually airlifts to a secure airfield.

Deployment by air necessitates the size and weight of an alert contingency MAGTF be kept to an absolute minimum. An alert contingency MAGTF may employ independently or in conjunction with amphibious, maritime prepositioning, or other expeditionary forces. The rapid deployment of the II MEF alert contingency MAGTF following the October 23, 1983, terrorist bombing of the US Marine Corps barracks in Lebanon, is an example of expeditionary agility by a SPMAGTF.

Task-Organised Outside the MAGTF

On occasion, US Marine Corps forces may task-organise to conduct operations outside of the MAGTF construct. These occasions usually occur when specific capabilities are required, singly or in concert with those provided by the other services and US Special Operations Command, to conduct operations that are narrow in purpose, scope, or duration or to provide a joint force commander, another component, or civil authorities complementary capabilities or additional capacity.

US Marine Corps fighter-attack squadrons, for example, are regularly assigned to carrier air wings to provide the additional capacity necessary to support rotational deployment of the US Navy's aircraft carriers.

Given geographic combatant commanders' growing requirements for similar engagement and protection activities, US Marine Corps assets may deploy from a variety of US Navy and Military Sealift Command ships. Deployments are undertaken to conduct security cooperation, provide foreign humanitarian assistance, and maritime security missions or to provide increased protection when those ships are transiting high-threat areas.

Another example is the Chemical Biological Incident Response Force (CBIRF) which provides a scalable response capability for MAGTF operations and may provide direct support to the geographic combatant commanders. For example, CBIRF responded to the 2001 anthrax incident in Washington DC. Whether capabilities are drawn from MAGTF assets or separate commands, task-organising US Marine Corps forces in nonstandard ways for employment in concert with a variety of partners requires the close involvement of the US Marine Corps component commanders. They play a key role in identifying geographic combatant commander and other component commander requirements - especially those of their navy and special operations counterparts - and developing innovative ways to meet them.

Left: **A CH-53E Super Stallion assigned to Marine Heavy Helicopter Squadron 772 (HMH-772) sling-loads a Humvee during an Integrated Training Exercise at Marine Air-Ground Combat Center, Twentynine Palms, California.** US Marine Corps/Captain Mark Andries

Left: **A CH-53E Super Stallion assigned to Marine Heavy Helicopter Squadron 361 (HMH-361) during a Service Level Training Exercise (SLTE) at Camp Wilson, Marine Corps Air-Ground Combat Center, Twentynine Palms, California. SLTE is a series of exercises designed to prepare a Marine Air-Ground Task Force for quick and effective responses to military operations.** US Marine Corps/ LCpl Richard Perez Garcia

MH-60R SEAHAWK CHARACTERISTICS

Primary function	Anti-Submarine Warfare, Surface Warfare Helicopter
Date deployed by US Navy	2006
Length	64ft 10in (19.76m)
Folded length	41ft (12.51m)
Width	53ft 8in (16.35m)
Folded width	11ft (3.35m)
Height	16ft 8in (5.10m)
Folded height	12ft 11in (3.94m)
Main rotor diameter	53ft 8in (16.35m)
Tail rotor diameter	11ft (3.35m)
Max take-off weight	23,500lb (10,659kg)
Empty weight	14,430lb (6.545kg)
Max speed	180kts
Ceiling	13,000ft (3,900m)
Range	245nm (453km)
Engines	Two GE T700-GE-401 each rated in the 1,800shp class
Crew	Two pilots and one aviation warfare systems operator

Data: Lockheed Martin

Operating the MH-60R

In US Navy service, an MH-60R is operated by a three-person crew consisting of two pilots and an aviation warfare systems operator. All US Navy MH-60R pilots must be proficient in flying the aircraft, the emergency procedures, how to perform the mission set, and be proficient at employing the helicopter's tactical sensors for surface and sub-surface warfare. The sensor suite includes an AQS-22 dipping sonar, an APS-153 multi-mode radar, ALQ-210 electronic support measures, and an AAS-44 multi-spectral targeting system.

The aviation warfare systems operator is at the helm of radar operations, conducts anti-submarine acoustic operations, deploys sonar buoys, manages the IFF tracks, and runs the infrared camera to target AGM-114 Hellfire missiles and AGR-20 guided rockets.

The mission set of an HSM squadron is split between anti-submarine (sub-surface) warfare, surface warfare, air warfare and electronic warfare. Each function has its own syllabus which for qualification purposes is broken down into separate grade sheets that all aircrew must complete.

Explaining the syllabus requirements, Lt Phillips said: "The MH-60 weapons school issues the syllabus requirements to the fleet squadrons. We work through each requirement during sorties. Sometimes it can take an entire flight to execute all the prerequisites and requirements to assess someone, sometimes more than one flight if the individual is less proficient."

As the pilot flying the mission, Lt Phillips said his focus is on the flight display and instruments helped by the automatic flight control system: "Realistically, the MH-60R's autopilot functions a lot differently to autopilots of fixed wing aircraft. We don't have a button to push that flies the helicopter at a certain level and direction, we are required to fly the aircraft in that way. Though my primary job is safety of flight, I can also view the tactical picture to gain an understanding of what's happening to assist the airborne tactics officer without dedicating my entire focus to that. For example, when descending for a sonar dipping pattern at 150 feet above the water and 120 knots the pilot is locked on to the altitude and airspeed figuring out how to set up the aircraft to best fly the dipping pattern. That's amplified at night. The pilot flies the same pattern but on goggles without any external references to help but uses

Below: **Sailors assigned to Helicopter Maritime Strike Squadron 74 (HSM-74) 'Swamp Foxes', prepare an MH-60R Seahawk helicopter for flight on the flight deck of aircraft carrier USS *Harry S Truman* (CVN 75).** US Navy/Mass Communication Specialist Lyle Wilkie III

Right: **An MH-60R Seahawk helicopter assigned to Helicopter Maritime Strike Squadron 74 (HSM-74) flies in front of the guided-missile cruiser USS *San Jacinto* (CG 56) during operations with units assigned to French Task Force 473. The aim of the operation was to enhance levels of cooperation and interoperability, enhance mutual maritime capabilities, and promote long-term regional stability in the US 5th Fleet area of responsibility.** Marine Nationale/ Chief Petty Officer Bruno Gaudry

Below: **An MH-60R Seahawk helicopter assigned to Helicopter Maritime Strike Squadron 74 (HSM-74) takes off from the aircraft carrier USS *Harry S Truman* (CVN 75), while underway in the Mediterranean Sea.** US Navy/Mass Communication Specialist Lyle Wilkie III

the sight picture and instruments in most sea states.

"With a heavy sea state, high winds, and a submarine below, the pilot and the crew must track it for the safety of the carrier strike group. That's an operational environment when pilot proficiency really counts. The heavier the sea state, the harder it is to maintain a stable hover. When you're trying to fight the aircraft and follow what the computer is telling you, it's a heavy workload."

Considering the low operating altitudes flown over the ocean and the environmental factors encountered, from extremely cold air to very humid warm air, Phillips continued: "The helicopter handles extremely well, the two General Electric T700-GE-401 engines provide plenty of power and torque. The pilot must know the density altitude and the pressure altitude, use charts to help determine how environmental factors will impact the helicopter's performance. The hotter and more humid it is, the greater the power demand on the engines to maintain the flight regime. That affects the pilot's ability to maintain certain angles of bank, and to hover at certain altitudes. In some situations when it's more difficult to take off, or to hover, the pilot must plan around those conditions by using operational risk management to assess the risk associated with the conditions. Is the aircraft able to perform at that level and am I willing to accept the associated risk at that point? We might have to burn down more fuel to decrease our weight: it all comes down to the pre-flight performance calculation and recognising what the aircraft limitations are. We rely on the pre-flight calculations and use the flight management system as a back-up."

In terms of strike capability Phillips said: "The Hellfire is our primary missile

MH-60R FEATURES

- Redundant flight control system
- Ballistically tolerant upper controls and hub
- 23mm ballistically tolerant main rotor blades
- Redundant fail-safe tail rotor controls
- Self-sealing fuel tanks
- High mass components retained in 20/20/10G crash conditions
- Modular transmission with fail-safe lubrication
- Triple redundant hydraulic and electrical system
- Spall-resistant windshield and cockpit structure
- Jettisonable cockpit windows
- Protective seating for all crew members
- Energy absorbing landing gear

Data: Lockheed Martin

and at the same time we also carry the Advanced Precision Kill Weapons System. Because of our varied mission set our loadouts differ to suit our tasking. We

MH-60R COCKPIT AVIONICS

- Four 8 x 10 in (20.3 x 25.4cm) full-colour flight and mission displays
- Digital communications suite
- Integrated global positioning satellite unit/inertial navigation system
- Mass memory data storage unit
- Ruggedised integrated mission computer
- Flight management computer and operations software
- Full-colour, night vision capable, sunlight readable glass cockpit common with the MH-60S helicopter

Data: Lockheed Martin

can carry a swing load, torpedoes, and missiles at the same time, which requires prioritisation and consequently minimises the ability to perform one mission or the other. For some missions, we might have a wingman, but for the most part, we operate alone and independent of the rest of the strike group."

An MH-60R can carry a significant amount of fuel which enables the helicopter to fly hundreds of miles away from the carrier and provide an extended sight picture. An MH-60R can land on the flight deck of various classes of ship to refuel, but if the sea state prevents a safe landing, the MH-60R crew has an aerial refuelling kit at their disposal.

Employing the kit while in a hover, the crew hoists up a fuel hose from the ship's flight deck, hooks it up to the aircraft and uploads fuel. Understandably the aerial refuelling procedure is more difficult when the ship is pitching and rolling.

Right and middle: **An MH-60R Seahawk helicopter assigned to the 'Swamp Foxes' of Helicopter Maritime Strike Squadron 74 (HSM-74), departs the flight deck of the guided-missile destroyer USS *Stout* (DDG 55) after a helicopter inflight refuelling.**
US Navy/Mass Communication Specialist Bill Dodge

Below: **An MH-60R Seahawk helicopter assigned to the Swamp Foxes of Helicopter Maritime Strike Squadron 74 (HSM-74) lifts off the flight deck of the aircraft carrier USS *Dwight D Eisenhower* (CVN 69) operating in the US 5th Fleet area of operations deployed in support of Operation Inherent Resolve.**
US Navy/Seaman Joshua Murray

Aircrewman

After a two-year training course, Clayton Loose graduated as a Naval Aircrewman Tactical Helicopter (AWR). He serves in an MH-60R crew as an aviation warfare systems operator. His graduation followed attendance at eight different schools, the first three of which are based at Naval Air Station Pensacola, Florida. Those schools are the Aircrew Candidate School (four weeks) to learn water and land survival skills and flight safety; the Rescue Swimmer School (five weeks) to learn search and rescue techniques; and the Class A Technical School (14 weeks) to study basic skills in naval aviation.

The course continues with Survival, Evasion, Resistance, and Escape school (two weeks) at Naval Air Station North Island, California or Naval Shipyard Portsmouth, New Hampshire, to train in SERE techniques, then a Fleet Replacement Squadron (28 weeks) for on-site aircraft systems training and to demonstrate competency in safety of flight, confidence, and a knowledge of all the mission capabilities: surface warfare, anti-submarine warfare, and electronic warfare.

There are two MH-60R Fleet Replacement Squadrons; HSM-40 'Air Wolves' assigned to Helicopter Maritime Strike Wing, US Atlantic Fleet based at Naval Station Mayport, Florida, and HSM-41 'Sea Hawks' which is assigned to Helicopter Maritime Strike Wing, US Pacific Fleet based at Naval Air Station North Island, California.

Discussing the FRS course, AWR Loose said: "The syllabus involves instruction in the capabilities and limitations of the aircraft [and] provides the first time a student gets hands-on with the aircraft's systems. We also complete plenty of simulator time. Each event flown on a simulator is graded. We complete several simulators before we fly a mission to gain proficiency, especially those in the

MH-60R SENSOR SYSTEMS

- Open, scalable, plug and play avionics architecture, capable of growth with minimal impact on current avionics systems
- Capable of launching eight AGM-114 Hellfire missiles from right and left extended pylons
- Integrated AAS-44 Forward-Looking Infrared (FLIR) system for expanded night vision and AGM-114 Hellfire missile targeting capability
- APS-153 multi-mode radar with long/short range search Inverse Synthetic Aperture Radar imaging and periscope detection modes
- Integrated AQS-22 Airborne Low Frequency Sonar with expanded littoral and deep-water capability, including concurrent dipping sonar and sonobuoy processing capability
- Military-off-the-shelf based mission and flight management computers
- ALQ-210 Electronic Support Measures (ESM) system for passive detection, location, and identification of emitters
- Sensor data integrated into actionable information provides threat assessment and superior situational awareness of the digital battlefield
- Data link for radar, FLIR, voice, acoustics, ESM, and mission display
- Integrated self defence system providing chaff and flare countermeasures, and self-protection for RF, IR, and Laser threats

Data: Lockheed Martin

tactical phase such as surface warfare and anti-submarine warfare. Each student flies on an MH-60R within the first two weeks of the FRS course."

The follow-on phase teaches students about vertical replenishment, air refuelling, and how to safely conduct emergency procedures. Air refuelling events take place with an MH-60R helicopter hovering above the flight deck of a ship.

During the refuelling process, aircrewmen communicate with the personnel on the ship's flight deck, acting as the liaison between the flight deck crew and the pilots up front. Directing the pilots to keep position relative to the ship while giving hand signals to the ship deck about what they need to do to bring in the fuelling hose, attaching it to the air refuelling nozzle located at the cabin door, and monitoring fuel flow. It's a busy procedure for the aircrewman.

Air refuelling training is conducted over a hover pad marked out like a ship's deck; weighted bag on the hoist being used to replicate the air refuelling nozzle. Aircrewmen run through standard communications and build hand-eye coordination of where they need to place the aircraft over the deck. AWR Loose noted that aircrewmen don't get any exposure to a ship at the FRS saying: "That only happens once you get to a fleet squadron.

"We also conduct search and rescue using the AAS-44 FLIR's infrared camera and learn how to set up the cabin configuration to enable the rescue in a timely manner, and we do not learn about the technicalities of the sensors until we join our first fleet squadron. Students are expected to demonstrate deep knowledge of the system, for example, understanding why the sensor is being used in the way it is. Students then transition to applying the sensors, a process that's aided using a simulator to undertake specific scenarios.

"Typically, anti-submarine warfare occupies the bulk of the training

Left: **An air crewman attaches a fuel line to an MH-60R Seahawk during a helicopter-in-flight refuelling exercise aboard the Ticonderoga-class guided-missile cruiser USS *Mobile Bay* (CG 53).** US Navy/Mass Communication Specialist 2nd Class Armando Gonzales

Below: **Sailors hold a fuel line during a helicopter-in-flight refuelling exercise aboard the Ticonderoga-class guided-missile cruiser USS *Mobile Bay* (CG 53) underway in the Red Sea.** US Navy/Mass Communication Specialist Armando Gonzales

Left: **Sailors heave in a fuel line during a hellcopter-In-flight refuelling exercise aboard the USS *Mobile Bay* (CG 53) underway in the Red Sea.** US Navy/Mass Communication Specialist Armando Gonzales

APS-153(V) MULTI-MODE MARITIME SURVEILLANCE RADAR

Telephonics' APS-153(V) capabilities include extremely small target detection, high-resolution imaging, and long-range surface search which support anti-submarine warfare, anti-surface warfare, C4ISR, surface surveillance, maritime interdiction, search and rescue, battle damage assessment, and naval surface fire support.

According to Telephonics, the radar operator can classify detected moving ship targets under night and restricted visibility using the high-resolution Inverse Synthetic Aperture Radar mode. This mode allows the MH-60R to operate outside of visual and lethal range of a potential enemy and to identify detected targets when images are combined with other intelligence.

As per its title, the APS-153(V) can operate in modes for maritime surveillance, ISAR imaging, small target/ automatic radar periscope detection and discrimination (ARPDD), short range search and rescue, navigation, and identification friend or foe (IFF).

The APS-153(V) is fully integrated into the cockpit avionics suite and controlled through the aircraft's mission computer with returns shown on cockpit multi-function displays, providing the crew with independent views of radar data. Shipboard personnel have virtually the same radar picture as the flight crew fed by the aircraft's C-band data link.

Below: **This photograph of an MH-60R Seahawk helicopter assigned to HSM-74 on the flight deck of guided-missile cruiser USS *Laboon* (DDG 58) was taken during flight operations in the Arabian Sea. The image clearly shows the AAS-44 Forward-Looking Infrared sensor turret fitted on the forward fuselage, and the under fuselage-mounted radome of the APS-153 multi-mode radar.** US Navy/Mass Communication Specialist Seaman Jeremy Boan

always changing, and you need to adapt to those ever-changing factors."

Maintenance

The MH-60R Seahawk helicopter undergoes maintenance inspections every seven, 14, and 28 days, and out to 546 days. Driven by the age of the aircraft and the number of hours accumulated, aircraft are inducted for depot level maintenance on a 42/28-month cycle.

According to Petty Officer Ramos, an aviation avionics technician (AT1) assigned to HSM-74, the inspections are complex: "If a main rotor blade needs to be replaced, the new blade must undergo a torque inspection and undergo testing on the deck and in the air. The aircraft cannot return to operations until a functional check flight is completed. Then, the logs and records must be completed stating that all the inspection checks met the requirements. Then, and only then can the aircraft return to operational flying. We try to plan months and months in advance to make sure we can operate throughout a deployment with the least amount of periodic maintenance inspections as is possible."

Discussing a potential engine change, Petty Officer Ramos suggests an engine can be swapped in four to five hours: "That depends on whether we're swapping the entire engine and its components or we're removing components for a quick engine change which involves swapping the main carcass of the engine. But that's not the entire timeline. From the time an engine is taken off the aircraft and a new engine is installed, we must return the aircraft back up to the flight deck or out to the flight line, complete the checks to ensure the engine runs satisfactorily on the deck/ground, and then in flight, troubleshoot any failures, takes two-and-a-half to three days."

timeline - it's the aircrewman's bread and butter task. When we're operating from a ship, our primary role is to protect the carrier. By using a mobile target tracker called an EMAT, we can mimic a submarine in the water which we can locate and track.

"At the end of the 28 weeks, we are issued with a final battle problem, a complex scenario featuring all events you've been graded on during the course, especially in the simulator during anti-submarine warfare: that's your final checkpoint prior to graduation.

"Once you've started on a fleet squadron, you enter the carrier work-up cycle, which involves greater numbers of aircraft operating in the battlespace, for which you must understand their capabilities, and more effectively conduct your mission.

"We constantly work with the carrier's combat information centre, HSM-74 has AWS rates who work in the centre to make the information fed in from an MH-60R, more intuitive to the other ratings who work in the centre. Similarly, we conduct

a lot of work with P-8 maritime patrol aircraft in the anti-submarine warfare role. The P-8 has a robust sensor suit, so the aircraft feeds us more amplifying information on battlespace activity.

"Once a newly trained aircrewman joins HSM-74, or any fleet squadron, they are continually being certified and re-qualified, it's a full-time job. The information is always changing, tactics are

support combat readiness and training of carrier air wings and strike groups.

The department comprises divisions:

Air Wing Intelligence Training is responsible for training CVW intelligence officers and enlisted intelligence specialists in strike support operations.

Targeting trains and certifies all carrier air wing targeting personnel and provides distributed reach-back support for deployed units worldwide regarding target development.

Command Information Services provides cyber security and computer network operations for the entire NAWDC enterprise.

Operations

NAWDC's Operations Department is responsible for the coordination, planning, synchronization, and scheduling for the operations of the command, its assigned aircraft, and airspace and range systems within the Fallon Range Training Complex.

Maintenance

NAWDC's Maintenance Department provides mission-ready fleet and adversary aircraft configured with the required weapons and systems for all training evolutions. The department supports day-to-day training missions with the F-16, F/A-18 Super Hornet,

F-35C Lightning II, EA-18G Growler, E-2C Hawkeye and the MH-60S Seahawk as well as conducting scheduled and unscheduled maintenance on the individual aircraft.

STRIKE

Responsible for training naval aviators in advanced TTPs across various combat mission areas at individual, unit, integrated, and joint levels, with an aligned training programme that is constantly being developed. Its objectives are to set and enforce combat proficiency standards, and to develop, validate, standardise, publish and revise TTPs.

NAWDC is a repository for naval aviation subject matter experts, so it uses that expertise to support strike group, numbered fleet, component, and combatant commanders by leading training events, assessing warfighting effectiveness, by identifying and mitigating gaps across all platforms and staffs for assigned mission areas, and collaborating with other warfighting development centres to ensure cross-platform integration and alignment.

CAEWWS

Carrier Airborne Early Warning Weapons School (CAEWWS), also referred to as

Above: **NAWDC's Airborne Electronic Attack Weapons School operates a handful of EA-18G Growler electronic attack aircraft.**
Mark Ayton

Left: **NAWDC has a couple of E-2C Hawkeye airborne early warning aircraft assigned for use by the Carrier Airborne Early Warning Weapons School.**
Mark Ayton

warfighting development centres and weapons schools.

CAEWWS also provides support to advanced integrated fleet training by way of WTI augmentation to the STRIKE department for Air Wing Fallon detachments.

TOPGUN

TOPGUN provides advanced tactics training for F/A-18 Super Hornet and F-35C Lightning II aircrew via the Strike Fighter Tactics Instructor (SFTI) course. TOPGUN is the most demanding air combat syllabus found anywhere in the world. The SFTI course produces graduate-level strike fighter tacticians, adversary instructors, and air intercept controllers who move to a fleet tour as a squadron training officer.

One important aspect of the TOPGUN weapons school is that it does not conduct the Strike Fighter Advanced Readiness Program (SFARP) for either the F/A-18 Super Hornet or the F-35C Lightning II. That programme is run by the satellite weapons schools located at Naval Air Station Lemoore, California (Strike Fighter Weapons School Pacific SFWSPAC) and Naval Air Station Oceana, Virginia (Strike Fighter Weapons School Atlantic SFWSLANT) using the syllabus that NAWDC creates. There is insufficient time available in the year for NAWDC to manage and run the SFARP programme.

The SFWSPAC and the SFWSLANT provide standardised graduate level training through curricula covering every aspect of F/A-18 weapons employment. Thirty weapons and tactics courses for strike fighter aircraft are taught on a continuing basis to fleet squadrons, reserve squadrons and naval air stations. The amount of ordnance uploaded in courses offered at the SFWSPAC totals over 2.5m pounds annually.

Helicopters

The Rotary Wing Weapons Schools each instruct a Seahawk Weapons and Tactics Instructor programme; provide tactics instructors to fleet squadrons; maintain and develop the navy's helicopter tactics doctrine; instruct the navy's mountain flying school; provide high-altitude, mountainous flight experience for sea-going squadrons; and provide academic, ground, flight, and opposing-forces instruction for visiting aircrew during Air Wing Fallon detachments.

The two weapons schools, SEAWOLF for the MH-60S and SEAHUNTER for the MH-60R, used to be combined under N8. SEAWOLF, the previous school was split because each Seahawk variant is significantly different: the airframe is similar, but the mission sub-systems and their capabilities are different.

Depending on aircraft and range availability, the MH-60 courses last between eight to nine weeks. On the MH-60R course, anti-submarine warfare takes up most of the flight events and simulator events.

Electronic warfare and weapons employment using the AGM-114 Hellfire

Below: **A slick F/A-18E Super Hornet configured for an air-to-air mission launches from runway 31L at Fallon on a sunny June afternoon.**
Mark Ayton

TOP DOME, is the E-2 weapon school and responsible for airborne tactical command and control advanced individual training via the Hawkeye Weapons and Tactics Instructors (HEWTIs) class.

CAEWWS is also responsible for development of TTPs, provides inputs to the acquisition process in the form of requirements and priorities for research and development (R&D), procurement, and training systems, and supports other

missile and the APKWS laser-guided rocket are also part of the course.

An overwater phase ties in with Resolute Hunter, an extensive exercise run by the MISR department and detailed later, takes place from Naval Air Station North Island. Students complete their simulators for the surface warfare phase and then participate in Resolute Hunter.

The course starts with an academic phase comprising lectures and a test followed by a surface warfare and an anti-submarine warfare phase, which both comprise simulator events and flights. An overland phase and weapons employment are tied together. All weapons employment is conducted over the Fallon range with simulator events scheduled for each of the robust scenarios. A mountain flying course is completed in the mountains near to Fallon.

Pointing out the downside of using the MH-60R for overland missions flown from Fallon, Lieutenant Scott Haeusler said: "The MH-60R is a maritime platform designed to operate over the water, its maritime radar has limited capabilities over land so we're operating with one hand tied behind our back because we don't have the situational awareness that our radar creates.

"NAWDC has no MH-60Rs assigned, just MH-60S helicopters. All the student pilots are qualified to fly the MH-60S, it has the same cockpit, so it's an easy transition, which they fly for proficiency. For the course we use fleet aircraft flown in from North Island, California, and from a location close to the range complex to be used for the over water missions.

"For part of the course, we switch between North Island and Naval Air Station Jacksonville in Florida. During the most recent course most of the ASW sims were completed at Jacksonville which were followed by further sims at North Island prior and during Exercise Resolute Hunter, which is always staged on the west coast.

"One notable event of the MH-60R WTI course staged during the spring of 2023 was the graduation of the first Australian student who is serving on an exchange tour with the US Navy."

Safety

The safety department serves as the principal advisor to the Commander on all matters pertaining to safe command operations and is responsible for administering safety programmes in aviation, ground, ergonomics, motor vehicles (personal and commercial), recreation, and on- and off-duty. Its primary objective is to eliminate preventable mishaps while maximising operational readiness.

HAVOC

The Airborne Electronic Attack Weapons School, call sign HAVOC is comprised of qualified Growler Tactics Instructors, or GTIs, who are the subject matter experts in the EA-18G community who develop

Below: **This F/A-18F was the only Super Hornet aircraft assigned to NAWDC at the time of the author's visit to Fallon painted in an aggressor colour scheme.**
Mark Ayton

the TTPs to get the most out of EA-18G sensors and weapons.

HAVOC trains Growler aircrew and intelligence officers on the TTPs during the biannual Growler Tactics Instructor Course, a rigorous 14-week syllabus of academic, simulator, and live fly events that earn graduates the GTI qualification.

The GTI course comprises academic, simulator and live flight events flown from Naval Air Station Fallon in the Fallon Range Training Complex and from Nellis Air Force Base in the Nevada Test and Training Range. There are three main phases each focused on electronic attack: air-to-air; air-to-ground including an AGM-88 HARM missile shoot; and participation in the integration phase of the US Air Force Weapons Instructor Course as the GTI course capstone event. When Growler aircraft deploy to and operate from Nellis the crews operate with multiple types, including F-22s, F-35s, and non-kinetic effects.

Course instruction focuses on current TTPs and the Growler's integration with joint forces and thorough debriefs of each event.

With service entry of the F-35C Lightning II strike fighter, the ability to employ non-kinetic effects for the SEAD role is no longer limited to EA-18G Growlers. Mission crossover exists such that the two types are different and complementary.

Maritime ISR

According to details published by Navy. mil, the MISR WTI programme was devised by US Navy Commander Peter Salvaggio during a deployment to the CENTCOM area of responsibility in 2010. His concept of creating a standalone environment where disaggregated platforms, weapons, sensors, and services could agnostically train together in a changing environment, was finally realised when the first MISR WTI course launched in October 2018,

followed by the first edition of Resolute Hunter in April 2019.

The US Navy created the MISR Weapons School and the MISR WTI syllabus for training sailors in high-end ISR integration, connecting sensors, weapons, and decision-makers across all domains, a necessity for developing accurate target packages.

MISR WTI students are primarily aviators including pilots of the MH-60R and MH-60S Seahawk helicopters, naval flight officers serving with EP-3E Aries and P-8A Poseidon aircraft, others, including enlisted sailors come from roles in the intelligence, cryptologic warfare, surface warfare, and maritime space communities, other students come from the US Marine Corps, the US Air Force, the Royal Australian Air Force, and the Royal Air Force.

The biannual course lasts for 18 weeks which graduate 20 students annually with the WTI qualification.

STRIKE

Editor of the US Navy and Marine Corps Yearbook, **Mark Ayton** spoke to Commander Michael Patterson, head of the STRIKE department about the Air Wing Fallon programme.

WIDELY RATED AS the best graduate level training programme available, Air Wing Fallon is staged by the Naval Aviation Warfighting Development Center's STRIKE department, which is equipped with the systems, ranges and instructors required to stage and run the five-week intensive training schedule. The STRIKE department's mission is to train carrier air wings to be ready for deployment.

Once Air Wing Fallon is complete, the CVW is declared surge ready but may not deploy for a month or two during which sustainment training maintains readiness. In that event, every 45 days or so, the air wing returns to the carrier to re-qualify in day and night-time landing proficiency.

Air Wing Fallon Training

NAWDC's primary mission is integrated training, both live and virtual, of air wings in the final phase of the Optimised Fleet Response Plan (OFRP). The focus is on TTPs tailored to fight and win a high-end fight against peer competitors.

To properly prepare aircrew for anticipated threats, NAWDC continually updates the threat emulators arranged on the Fallon Range Training Complex (FRTC), the Air Wing Fallon syllabi, and its training systems and facilities. However, NAWDC has outgrown the FRTC, so the command is expanding the airspace to the south and east of the current range. It's also using airspace altitude reservations between the FRTC and the Utah Test and Training Range, to the east, and the Nevada Test and Training Range, to the south. The command is also using Live, Virtual and Constructive (LVC) training to complement the airspace structure.

After its first year of operation, NAWDC's new integrated training facility (ITF) provides the ability to conduct the full scope of Air Wing Fallon integrated training at the security levels required to employ the full capabilities of the CVW and train for a high-end fight.

The ITF will integrate with other navy sites through the Navy Continuous Training Environment which enables LVC

Below: **E-2D BuNo 169231/ AJ601 assigned to Carrier Airborne Early Warning Squadron 124 (VAW-124) 'Bear Aces' seen on take-off from Naval Air Station Fallon during Air Wing Fallon for Carrier Air Wing 8 in February 2023.** Dan Stijovich

training with live and synthetic systems around the globe. This enables various training events including joint mission rehearsal, integrated strike group air defence training, Air Wing Fallon mission rehearsal, weapons, and tactics instructor support, TTP development, combatant commander mission rehearsal, and unit-level training.

In its preparation for deployment, the air wing starts with small unit exercises practising skills to make pilots effective in the cockpit, or maybe as a basic fighting element such as a section [a two-ship] or a division [a four-ship] of F/A-18s or F-35s.

Below: **F/A-18E Super Hornet BuNo 166783/ AJ331 at Fallon in February 2023 during Air Wing Fallon. The aircraft is configured with a single aerial refuelling pod on the centreline station.**
Dan Stijovich

From there, the air wing goes on to a slightly more complex training evolution where they go to the ship for an event known as Tailored Ship's Training Availability (TSTA). That's a chance for the air wing to exercise with the ship, build working relationships and operate together - that's key to their success.

Once TSTA is complete, the air wing deploys to Naval Air Station Fallon for the five-week Air Wing Fallon detachment, run by NAWDC's STRIKE department. To put that in context, after the air wing leaves Fallon, it goes back to the ship for COMPTUEX which lasts roughly a month. COMPTUEX involves the entire carrier strike group, the carrier, the guided missile destroyers, cruisers, and the air wing operating and training together for certification. Once the carrier strike group, including its air wing, has successfully completed COMPTUEX, it is certified to deploy.

Air Wing Fallon brings all the air wing's elements together to mission plan, fly from Fallon to operate on the FRTC to conduct each mission set conducted by each type in the air wing. The building blocks for executing each mission set come from the respective weapons school.

Explaining the input the STRIKE department has on Air Wing Fallon,

Above: **Midway through the landing gear retraction cycle, the pilot of F/A-18E Super Hornet BuNo 166832/AJ104 assigned to Strike Fighter Squadron 37 (VFA-37) 'Bulls' heads out to the Fallon range.**
Dan Stijovich

Commander Michael Patterson, STRIKE department head said: "It is probably the first time the entire air wing has come together in its work-up cycle. Bear in the mind, the skills required for F/A-18s to work with Growlers, to work with Hawkeyes, to work with helicopters, and F-35s, are unique. The scenarios and skills required are different to those practiced by a squadron every day: an F/A-18 working with another F/A-18, is unit level training. At Air Wing Fallon, the term that we use is integration, how do you take one platform and use it to compensate for the weaknesses of another? How do you put them all together so that they're more than the sum of their parts? That is what we teach them during Air Wing Fallon.

"We start with a lecture series that takes about two days. The entire air wing undertakes one series of academics, and the mission commander candidates undertake different series of academics that are tailored toward qualifying as a mission commander, which is the top qualification earned by a pilot. It demonstrates their ability to lead the entire air wing on a strike mission. At the individual pilot level, we teach how to do conduct a strike and we also teach the mission commander candidates how to plan, execute and lead strike missions. The two levels of instruction happen simultaneously.

"Then there's a demo phase, where we show the air wing the mission planning process that we use at NAWDC. We show them an example of how to lead an air wing on a mission. From there, we hand the keys over and let the air wing run with it for the rest of the detachment, when instructors assigned to NAWDC embed with them while functioning as the White Force.

"STRIKE staff teach integration and are from multiple types, so they have the experience to operate as the White Force which manages mission execution. Most

Right: **EA-18G BuNo 166943/AJ500 assigned to Electronic Attack Squadron 142 (VAQ-142) 'Gray Wolves' enters the pattern at Fallon after an Air Wing Fallon mission.**
Dan Stijovich

Left: **Strike Fighter Squadron 213 (VFA-213) 'Black Lions' operates the F/A-18F model Super Hornet. It was the first fleet squadron to field the APG-79 AESA radar.**
Dan Stijovich

instructors assigned to STRIKE are F/A-18, some are F-35, and some are Growler, but during Air Wing Fallon we utilise Hawkeye and MH-60 instructors from the other NAWDC departments as augmentees to the STRIKE staff."

From an instructor standpoint, during Air Wing Fallon, STRIKE resembles a miniature air wing. All its instructors are embedded with the Blue Air, the White Cell, and with the opposing Red Air force in the daily events executed by the air wing. This enables instructors to observe first-hand what's going well and what's not going well, so they can determine what to do to help the air wing. Multiple screens display what's happening on the range.

Cdr Patterson said: "We can see how the Blue Air is doing, how the air wing is doing, and direct Red Air. After every flight event, once the maintenance actions are discussed with the maintenance department, all participating aircrew spend a couple of hours reviewing their tapes to gather the information that shows what they did during the flight and submit it to a member of the STRIKE staff.

"About two-and-a-half to three hours after the flight event ends, we start a mass debrief. Everybody participates, aircrew, mission planners and intelligence officers providing the intel support to the event. We watch the entire event. We go through

it and figure out whether the Blue Air achieved its mission, who died, who didn't.

"As we're going through the mission, we pull up the learning points. Maybe they had a bad game plan from the start so their performance on the range was not executed properly, or maybe they had a good game plan, but they didn't execute it properly for a myriad of reasons. We nit-pick all the good and all the bad things that they did and instruct them how to do it better next time. Each single event has a lengthy debrief process. At the end of week three, four, and then five [the end of the detachment] we collate all information into an executive overview for the air wing and the individual squadrons' leaders, so

Below: **EA-18G BuNo 168271/ AJ503 assigned to Electronic Attack Squadron 142 (VAQ-142) 'Gray Wolves' seen on take-off from Fallon during CVW-8's Air Wing Fallon detachment in February 2023. The snow-covered mountains in the background give a wintry impression of the high desert in northern Nevada.**
Dan Stijovich

they know how their pilots, aircrew and mission commander candidates did.

"The basis of the evaluation leans more to what they're doing on the range but issues that affect their missions are noted. If maintenance doesn't have the jets ready in time, if they're not fuelled in time, if they're not configured properly, or if they're not loaded out with the appropriate training ordnance, any one of these issues affects their missions. Similarly, with the game plan. Did the mission commanders allocate enough time to essentially get all the aircraft ready to launch out to the area in time? That's part of the game plan. Ultimately, we can't simulate all the other complications that the ship can present, they'll get that later."

In the final week, the air wing conducts three long-range strikes over the Pacific Ocean. They can be likened to capstone events and add additional factors, primarily flight time and distance to the operating area. These are complicating factors because the mission commanders must figure out how long it's going to take to get all the aircraft out to the operating area. The distances usually require aerial refuelling from big wing tankers or, less frequently F/A-18 tankers in the air wing.

Discussing the over water missions, Cdr Patterson said: "Missions conducted over the ocean are best done [actually] over the water for several reasons; the mountains around the Fallon range aren't a good replication of the ocean or our sensor application, and of course for the extra space available to us.

"Even though each event is large with 20 to 30 plus aircraft involved, that's not the air wing's full complement of aircraft so we conduct multiple long-range overwater

Right: **Strike Fighter Squadron 87 (VFA-87) 'Golden Warriors' is one of two squadrons assigned to CVW-8 equipped with the F/A-18E single-seat variant.** Dan Stijovich

Middle: **Strike Fighter Squadron 213 (VFA-213) F/A-18F Super Hornet BuNo 168930/ AJ213 is the commander's aircraft and has additional markings applied.** Dan Stijovich

Below: **A CMV-22B Osprey assigned to Fleet Logistics Multi-Mission Squadron 30 (VRM-30) 'Titans' fuels a MH-60S Seahawk helicopter (out of shot) during an air delivered ground refuelling evolution en route to participate in Air Wing Fallon.** US Navy/Chief Mass Communication Specialist Shannon Renfroe

strike missions so that each member of the air wing has an opportunity to see each mission type at least once, preferably twice. This enables them to learn from the first one and hopefully improve their performance on the second."

Unsurprisingly, strike missions involve dropping ordnance, live and inert.

During an Air Wing Fallon detachment, the air wing tends to drop more inert munitions simply because the targets that look more realistic on a sensor and are more threat representative are for inert weapons only. They tend to drop heavy inert munitions filled with concrete, not explosives. Additionally, during a five-week detachment, an air wing drops upwards of 30 JDAMs and employs a lot of simulated ordnance.

Integrating the F-35C

Discussing the fleet introduction of the F-35C Lightning II and its impact on the STRIKE department, Cdr Patterson said: "Its stealth characteristics, sensor fusion and the type of sensors is unique. Naval aviation already possessed some aspects of the F-35 in other platforms, but having all the aspects together in one aircraft brings new capabilities. It's a very capable aircraft, but it's not everything we want. It's got a lot of room for growth, and there's a lot of growth that it needs to have.

"Introduction of any new type-model-series, or for that matter, any

Left: **Sailors assigned to Helicopter Sea Combat 4 (HSC-4) 'Black Knights' install a GAU-21 0.50 calibre machine gun on a MH-60S Seahawk helicopter prior to a live fire training exercise during Air Wing Fallon.** US Navy/Mass Communication Specialist Ryan Breeden

new hardware or software capability on any type requires us to develop TTPs. How do we use the new capability to our best ability to enhance the air wing's capabilities? Our role is to devise how to use the new capability, a responsibility that generally falls to the specific weapons school that owns the type.

"The F-35C falls under TOPGUN. For us at STRIKE, the challenge is how we mesh the F-35C and its TTPs into the rest of the air wing. That's essential because the F-35C does not operate separately. If you keep it separate, you're not going to reap the maximum benefit from it. The F-35 was challenging because it performs similar roles to an F/A-18 and similar roles to a Growler, but it does them very differently.

So how do we weave those two together? How do we make the air crew talk to each other and understand the differences in capabilities and limitations? And then how do we match those up so that the strengths of the F-35 offset the weaknesses of an F/A-18? That was the challenge and role."

Discussing how the F-35C increases the combat effectiveness of an air wing, Cdr Patterson said: "An F-35-equipped air wing can do the things a non-F-35 air wing can do but do them better. We at STRIKE saw that when F-35-equipped Carrier Air Wing 2 was recently deployed here for Air Wing Fallon. We had to make our threat presentations more robust, to challenge them, because if not, they would shoot

Below: **A MH-60S Seahawk helicopter assigned to HSC-4 'Black Knights' approaches a landing zone during a live fire training exercise as part of Air Wing Fallon.** US Navy/Mass Communication Specialist Ryan Breeden

everyone down. We had to up our game on the adversary side to make sure we maintained the training value for them. That meant using F-35s on the Red Air side to meet the F-35's level of capability on the Blue Air side and fly the Red Air F-16s and Super Hornets smarter and harder.

"There's never going to be an air wing comprising all F-35s, at least that isn't going to exist in my lifetime. So as great as the aeroplane is, there's just never going to be enough of them. So how do you incorporate them into the rest of the air wing? How do you make the F-35 most effective?"

The author asked Commander Patterson if an air wing with two assigned F-35 squadrons were to undertake Air Wing Fallon in the years to come, would that further affect the training given the greater capability with more F-35s?

Cdr Patterson replied: "By the time that occurs, something else will have changed the threat. However, when VFA-147 completed Air Wing Fallon in 2019 it had fewer aircraft assigned than VFA-97 had this year. Consequently, VFA-97 operated a little bit differently to VFA-147. Whether it's an F-35-equipped air wing or not, we make the missions as hard as we possibly can, with a goal that the missions are harder than what future real-life missions would be. We don't run Air Wing Training Fallon to fail, we want to get the air wing over the line. It's our goal to make them ready for combat when they leave Fallon."

VISIT OUR ONLINE SHOP

FOR OUR FULL RANGE OF **MILITARY AVIATION** SPECIAL MAGAZINES

Key Shop

shop.keypublishing.com/specials

A
ffectionately known as the Warthog (or just plain 'Hog') the Fairchild Republic A-10 Thunderbolt II is one of the most distinctive aircraft in the USAF arsenal. This eagerly awaited special looks at a modern classic that first appeared in the seventies and has been widely used in Iraq, Afghanistan, and the Middle East.

F
rom Artem Mikoyan's 25hp Oktyabrenok of 1937 to the Mach 2.8-capable MiG-31 Foxhound and the next generation of 21st century MiG-35s, this 100-page special publication is a tribute to the designers, engineers and crews who have created, operated, and flown the most famous of Soviet military aircraft.

I
t remains the world's most successful fourth-generation fighter. Combat proven in roles that include air defence, air interdiction, close air support and suppression and destruction of enemy air defences, the F-16 remains at the forefront of air force inventories on each continent of the world.

E
xamining the US pivot from counter insurgency and asymmetric warfare to peer competition, and at the growing focus on the Pacific region, USAF Fighter Roadmap considers what the plan means for the nation's fighter requirements.

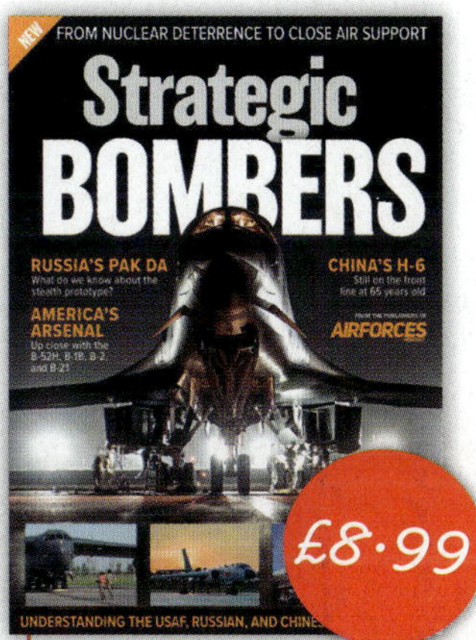

R
ussia's invasion of Ukraine and the subsequent drawn out war in Europe's southeastern corner has forced European air forces to rapidly reconfigure and re-orientate to face a peer-level threat that many believed had disappeared at the end of the Cold War.

L
egendary but no longer in service, the A-6 Intruder was the US Navy and US Marine Corps' primary attack aircraft for 30 years. Its maximum bomb payload was 18,000lb. A-6 Intruder tells the story of the aircraft including numerous accounts by US naval aviators of flying the jet in peacetime and in war from 1963 to 1997.

T
he term 'strategic bomber' is epitomised by the eight-engine B-52 Stratofortress. Even today, 71 years after its first flight, the B-52 is still top of the bill of aircraft designed and built for delivering munitions. This much-anticipated special lifts the lid on them, Strategic Bombers (Nuclear Deterrence to Close Air Support) is an essential read.

T
he publication also looks back over the past year at major operations and exercises involving British military aviation, missions around Ukraine and major NATO exercises, as well as looking developments in air warfare tactics and new technology.

FREE P&P* when you order online at...

shop.keypublishing.com/specials

Call +44 (0)1780 480404 *(Monday to Friday 9am-5.30pm GMT)*

Also available from **W.H Smith** and all leading newsagents. Or download from **Pocketmags.com** or your native app store - search *Aviation Specials*

*Free 2nd class P&P on all UK & BFPO orders. Overseas charges apply.

TOPGUN
TRAINING THE BEST OF THE BEST

Mark Ayton provides an overview of the US Navy's TOPGUN weapons school based at Naval Air Station Fallon, Nevada.

NO OTHER ELEMENT of US naval aviation is quite as famous as TOPGUN. Until Paramount Pictures released the movie *Top Gun* in 1986, featuring the F-14 Tomcat, few people had even heard of the unit. Millions of people around the world flocked to the cinema to watch 110 minutes of sheer Hollywood action, emerging with an impression of how selected US naval fighter pilots train to earn the coveted red patch awarded by the TOPGUN school to graduates who make the grade after three-plus months of gruelling flight operations.

Just like the days when the fictional Maverick and Iceman flew their F-14 Tomcats to the edge while operating from Naval Air Station Miramar near San Diego, then home to the TOPGUN weapons school, today highly talented navy fighter pilots still ply the same trade. But they do so with two marked differences. One, they fly either an F/A-18 Super Hornet or an F-35C Lightning II strike fighter aircraft, and they do so over northern Nevada, from the desert-bound Naval Air Station Fallon.

The TOPGUN weapons school provides advanced tactics training for F/A-18 Super Hornet and F-35C Lightning II aircrew via the 13-week Strike Fighter Tactics Instructor (SFTI) course. TOPGUN is deemed to be the most demanding air combat syllabus found anywhere in the world which produces graduate-level strike fighter tacticians, adversary instructors, and air intercept controllers who move to a fleet tour as a squadron training officer.

TOPGUN continually evolves, its staff are always looking to change driven by the introduction of a new aeroplane, most recently the F-35, or a new capability that's driven by a software or hardware upgrade to one type of aircraft, or more frequently because the threat has changed in some way, maybe different behaviour, maybe a new aircraft or a new weapon capability.

Commenting on the evolutionary nature of the TOPGUN weapons school, Commander Michael Patterson, a former department head said: "TOPGUN flexes to any such threat or threats, and within a matter of weeks or months, or maybe a year, its staff will develop a tactic to counter whatever the threat change is, then the school starts teaching on the changes to its students."

In May 2020, Major Derek Heinz, US Marine Corps and Lieutenant William Goodwin III, US Navy were the first two F-35C pilots to graduate from the TOPGUN course, Class 02-20. In doing so they were the first pilots to graduate TOPGUN in a new type of fighter since Super Hornet aircrew graduated for the first time from Class 05-01.

Integration of the F-35C to the TOPGUN school marked another significant change for the schoolhouse. It was no longer a course purely for legacy-type

Below: **All TOPGUN classes use augmenting, fleet representative aircraft deployed to Fallon by fleet squadrons. This photo shows six Super Hornets on the flight line from five different fleet squadrons.**
Mark Ayton

strike fighters, but one that caters for the new-generation systems integrated on the F-35C, with stealth capability.

In a press release issued at the time that the first two F-35C pilots graduated the TOPGUN school, the US Navy said: "Major Derek Heinz from the Rough Raiders and Lieutenant William Goodwin, III from the Argonauts successfully completed the 13-week Navy Strike Fighter Tactics Instructor [SFTI] course at the Naval Aviation Warfighting Development Center at Naval Air Station Fallon, Nevada. The SFTI course, otherwise known as TOPGUN, is an individual-level training course loaded with classroom lectures and labs, as well as simulated and live-fly events that are focused on the newest advanced tactical recommendations, and designed to create newly-minted tactics instructors who are ready to return and train the fleet."

TOPGUN department head, Commander Timothy Myers said: "Our focus on the students that go through TOPGUN is not limited to teaching them the tactics, techniques, and procedures that are required for them to successfully employ their aircraft, integrated into a larger force.

We are also in the business of teaching our graduates how to instruct other students so that when they go back to the fleet, they can instruct at a very high level.

"For the last few years, NAWDC and TOPGUN have been working to develop the skill-sets, curriculum, and experienced instructors required to execute a syllabus that fully integrates F-35C tactics, techniques, and procedures. While all F-35C tactics instructors have completed the TOPGUN course previously, this is the first time TOPGUN has graduated students who are currently flying the Lightning II, utilising a syllabus that has been developed, from the ground up, specifically for F-35C integrated operations. This was accomplished by the gradual introduction of F-35C tactics into the training curriculum for previous classes. The result is a cadre of highly-trained instructors executing a fully-integrated F-35C syllabus, providing well-rounded graduate-level training for the fifth-generation fighter to take back to the fleet.

"Graduating Strike Fighter Tactics Instructors allows us to accelerate learning by feeding TOPGUN training

Right: **Launching from runway 31L at Naval Air Station Fallon, Nevada, this F/A-18F is loaded with inert Joint Direct Attack Munitions for a TOPGUN air-to-surface mission.**
Mark Ayton

Below: **An F/A-18F on loan to TOPGUN from Strike Fighter Squadron 41 (VFA-41) 'Black Aces' loaded with inert Joint Direct Attack Munitions ahead of an air-to-surface mission in Phase 2 of the SFTI course.**
Mark Ayton

back to the fleet, elevating the lethality and survivability of both the individual aircraft as well as the Carrier Strike Group. The Lightning II proved its value to the navy during every phase of the TOPGUN course, and its integration with the F/A-18 Super Hornet, EA-18G Growler and E-2C/D Hawkeye demonstrated that the powerful combination of fourth and fifth generation fighters, with advanced electronic attack, and command and control, is a force-multiplier against advanced threats."

Lt Goodwin said: "Our focus is on assisting the SFTIs at the operational fleet squadron pushing the big picture tactics and ensuring that everything is ready to go for the first and subsequent F-35C carrier deployments. The idea is that VFA-147 SFTIs can use the standards of tactical execution we provide to train their own people and take that knowledge with them through deployment. We are here to ensure that they are set up for success."

Maj Heinz said: "While my role as an F-35C instructor is still primarily focused on the students at the Fleet Replacement Squadron [VFA-125], my perspective on what I teach and how I teach it most certainly has grown since completing TOPGUN. I'm still training students to fly the aircraft, it's just now I have the additional responsibility as an SFTI to bring that advanced training to the fleet, while helping maintain the TOPGUN training syllabus and ensuring standardisation of training for all instructors. We are always working to maintain the highest standards of training."

Course Phases

TOPGUN runs three courses per year. Each course lasts for about 12 weeks, with a month off in between, during which TOPGUN staff generally complete their own internal training.

Each SFTI course is divided into four phases. It includes academics, briefing labs, simulators, and flights. Students spend the first week in lectures run by TOPGUN staff who instruct about F-35 systems and capabilities, and threat systems and capabilities.

Explaining the individual phases, Cdr Patterson said: "Phase 1 is approximately two weeks of basic fighter manoeuvring (BFM). Despite the use of the word basic, it's complex one v one dogfighting. The top ten navy instructors are arguably

Below: **Strike Fighter Squadron 41 (VFA-41) 'Black Aces' based at Naval Air Station Lemoore, California loaned its CAG-bird F/A-18F for the TOPGUN class running in June 2023.** Mark Ayton

the best dog fighters in the fleet by a significant margin. When a student arrives at TOPGUN they may be quite good, but rarely are they ever good enough to be a TOPGUN instructor. So, the BFM phase provides a chance for the students to practice fighting against a pilot who is exquisitely good in the aeroplane. Consequently, the students improve their skills at fighting their aircraft in high G engagements. The BFM phase is usually undertaken on detachment to another location, somewhere closer to sea level, where the air is a little denser, and the aircraft perform better. Fallon is at a high elevation, so the aircraft perform differently when they're at higher elevation.

"Upon return to Fallon, students move on to Phase 2 air-to-surface weapon employment involving a week of academics learning about air-to-surface weapon employment, and practising air-to-surface weapons employment against threat representative targets and systems. After the air-to-surface phase, students move on to Phase 3 section air-to-air missions involving more academics and several weeks of simulators and flying section air-to-air missions, involving two aircraft, with the student leading an instructor operating as the wingman while evaluating the student in many scenarios. From there, students move to Phase 4 division air-to-air missions, involving four aircraft, in missions against multiple fighters.

"Interspersed with the air-to-air missions are integration missions, also air-to-air scenarios, involving other platforms, not least the EA-18G Growler, which requires unique skills. Towards the end of the course, students start conducting larger missions involving other types of aircraft, which involve mission planning. These events are like those staged for Air Wing Fallon but involve fewer aircraft integrating with other platforms."

One unique event of each TOPGUN class is called grad 1 v 1. It's a day of flight operations that has nothing to do with course graduation. Regardless of whatever phase of the course the pilots are in, the missions flown are all 1 v 1 dogfighting scenarios for which NAWDC brings in as

many types of aircraft it possibly can, from the US Air Force, the US Marines Corps, and the US Navy.

Explaining, Cdr Patterson said: "You take off, fly to a spot on the range at a certain altitude at a certain time, but you don't know who or what you're going to fight. So, you show up at that merge and it might be another F/A-18, an air force F-16, a navy F-16, maybe a Raptor, a Royal Air Force Typhoon, you don't know until you get there and see your opponent. You must react accordingly because each aeroplane has its own strengths and weaknesses. They finish the day with a talk by a combat veteran who speaks about their experiences, usually a MiG killer from the Vietnam war or Desert Storm.

Student Selection Process

Any candidate pilot wanting to go to TOPGUN must meet several requirements. Identifying two of the primary requirements, Cdr Patterson said: "Candidates must have maxed out their qualifications in the fleet, qualified as a division lead, and they need to have a certain number of flight hours, and experience in the aircraft.

"They submit their application to the TOPGUN staff, including a written statement explaining why they have a passion for the mission, why they think they'll be able to contribute to the community, and recommendations from an officer who has previously worked with the applicant stating whether they think the applicant would be successful, and able to get through the course or not. More importantly, will the applicant be a good representation of a TOPGUN graduate in their years removed from the course?

"Sometimes, if time and schedules allow, applicants will come to Fallon and complete a briefing lab with a staff member or a simulator or flight. That gives the staff member a chance to evaluate the candidate pilot on their abilities in flying the aeroplane, and their ability to teach. When a TOPGUN graduate returns to the fleet, they are expected to be good at flying and fighting the aircraft, and good at teaching other pilots to be good at flying and fighting the aircraft as well. They need to be able to raise the bar amongst all aircrew. Learning how to do that on a squadron is an integral part of the TOPGUN syllabus.

"When a student leads a flight, they must brief the mission. Briefing is deemed as one form of teaching. During

> "TOPGUN is constantly changing. It's full of young lieutenants that are smart and motivated, and never willing to settle for good enough. They're always trying to figure something out. They're always nit picking at each other, at themselves. And whatever the product is, whether it be their students, or tactics, they're constantly evolving."
>
> **COMMANDER MICHAEL PATTERSON**

Above: **An F/A-18E Super Hornet assigned to Strike Fighter Squadron 151 (VFA-151) 'Vigilantes' participated in the TOPGUN class running in June, 2023. The aircraft is seen at Fallon carrying an aerial refuelling pod on the centreline station and an inert Joint Direct Attack Munition.** Mark Ayton

Right: **Strike Fighter Squadron 147 (VFA-147) 'Argonauts' loaned three F-35Cs to the TOPGUN school for the class running in June, 2023. The aircraft shown is seen landing at Naval Air Station Lemoore, home station of VFA-147.**
Mark Ayton

Below: **Loaded with an air combat manoeuvring instrumentation pod and an inert AIM-9 Sidewinder missile, but no external fuel tanks, this slick F/A-18F is seen on take-off at Fallon bound for an air-to-air mission on the Fallon Range Training Complex.**
Mark Ayton

a briefing, a TOPGUN instructor can judge how good the student is at teaching and determine whether they are clearly communicating complex concepts to the instructor?

"Post mission, the student leads the debrief which is the event where so much learning occurs. The instructor wants to see if the student can pull out all the learning points, if they find all the things that went wrong, and are they teaching how to correct them in the future? So, the student is being evaluated and given feedback on how they are performing as an instructor for every event they do."

After a student has graduated from the TOPGUN course, they re-join their squadron as the WTI where they must maintain their instructor qualifications. Anytime a new tactic is developed it is promulgated to all strike fighter squadrons, via classified means, so that the squadron WTIs can learn about the new tactic.

Once a year, TOPGUN holds a conference called re-blue for which every TOPGUN graduate serving in the fleet is invited back to Fallon to spend two- or three-days attending lectures of all the new developments in threats and TTPs. Additionally, when TOPGUN conducts detachments to the various fleet bases, the instructors have an opportunity to interact with fleet operators, including TOPGUN graduates, to bring them up to speed on things that have changed.

One other significant role for instructors serving on the TOPGUN staff, is appointment as a subject matter expert. Not just for TOPGUN, but the entire navy. One example is the subject matter expert for the F/A-18 Super Hornet's radar. The process to become a subject matter expert takes up to 12 months of research. This involves visits to industry and their counterparts in the US Air Force, and the US Marine Corps, to increase the instructor's level of knowledge to prepare them for taking on the role.

In addition to the US Navy and Department of Defense intelligence communities providing TOPGUN with current information and guidance about the latest and emerging threats around the world, TOPGUN has subject matter experts who are very knowledgeable on a threat system, such as an air-to-air missile, aircraft, tactics, surface-to-air missile system. They acquire their knowledge by visiting the various intelligence communities to speak with analysts that specifically study that threat system. As they become more established and recognised for their knowledge in the broader intelligence community, they are regularly contacted by intelligence agencies to discuss new threats.

TRAINING WARRIORS, DEVELOPING LEADERS

Mark Ayton spoke with members of Training Air Wing 6 about the syllabus used for instructing Naval Flight Officers at Pensacola.

TRAINING AIR WING 6 based at Naval Air Station Pensacola, Florida is the US Navy's only Naval Flight Officer (NFO) training unit.

The command has three component training squadrons: VT-4 'Warbucks', VT-10 'Wildcats', and VT-86 'Sabrehawks'.

VT-4 conducts advanced student NFO training for students selected for the E-2 Hawkeye, E-6 Mercury, EP-3E Aries, and P-8A Poseidon aircraft with multi-crew simulators; VT-10 conducts primary and intermediate student NFO training with the T-6A Texan II aircraft; and VT-86

Above: **The T-45C Goshawk-equipped Training Squadron 86 (VT-86) 'Sabrehawks' conducts undergraduate strike naval flight officer training for the US Navy, US Marine Corps, and select international military partners.** US Navy/Captain Scott Janik

conducts advanced student NFO training with the T-45C Goshawk.

Wildcats

VT-10 is the navy's only primary NFO training squadron. Students arrive on the squadron having completed basic flight indoctrination flying civilian-registered Cessna aircraft at Pensacola.

Explaining the course, Commander Jason Agostinelli, commanding officer VT-10 said: "We have four stages for primary training: familiarisation, instruments, operational navigation and formation. Ground school comprises three weeks of lectures learning about the T-6A systems, and the

basics of the aircraft. They then start the familiarisation stage, flying the aircraft doing basic manoeuvres, landing patterns, radio calls, aerobatics, all to get a feel for the aircraft. Familiarisation is followed by instruments, which is the longest stage. The instruments stage starts with ground school learning about instrument navigation, getting the aircraft from point A to point B, using the instruments.

"Students get a lot of training in the simulators before they even get to the aircraft. Most of our simulator instructors are former military pilots and NFO instructors, which is a huge benefit to us. Using the simulator

Left: **Two T-45C Goshawk aircraft assigned to Training Squadron 86 (VT-86) 'Sabrehawks' over fly the white beaches of the Emerald Coast near Pensacola, Florida.** US Navy/ Captain Scott Janik

can be unscripted. if you need to take a student back and do another three-hour session, you can, and it's additional to what was planned. The split between simulator and aircraft is around 55:45. There's a little more simulator training to make sure the student has grasped the concepts, because it's a lot different when you're moving at 300 knots.

"We don't do a whole lot of VFR [visual flight rules] flying but do a lot of instrument flying, to get to our areas where they practice events like aerobatics and emergency procedures. When they return to the field here at Pensacola, they do some VFR flying to get into a landing pattern or when practicing an emergency approach.

"For an NFO, the instrument phase is not of primary importance. It provides an opportunity to learn the foundation of how you undertake normal procedure navigation, navigate through airways, and how you communicate with the instructor and with ATC agencies. It also sets a strong foundation for aviation and how it works.

"As an NFO, you'll never be alone in an aircraft, so you're always working with someone else, exercising crew resource management to get the job done, so a lot of what we do involves learning to be a member of a crew."

The operational navigation and formation stages follow instruments. All students complete both stages but in the order that best suits student loading at the time.

Explaining, Cdr Agostinelli said: "Operational navigation is low-level navigation where they navigate from point-to-point, figuring out how they get to the next point in the amount of time planned. It requires the student to manage their fuel, time, and weather.

"The formation stage, comprising three flights, introduces the student to flying with a wing man, a skill they will experience if they follow the strike fighter route."

Below: **T-6A BuNo 165996/F996 seen taxiing out to the main runway at Naval Air Station Pensacola on a primary NFO training flight.** Mark Ayton

Right: **T-45C BuNo 163622/ F609 assigned to Training Squadron 86 (VT-86) 'Sabrehawks' taxies back to its parking spot at Naval Air Station Pensacola on a primary NFO training flight.**
Mark Ayton

Below: **The crew of a T-6A Texan II prepare their respective cockpits prior to an afternoon mission from Naval Air Station Pensacola.**
Mark Ayton

If a student is selected for strike, they stay with VT-10 for an additional ten weeks for an intermediate strike syllabus, comprising 18 flights. The term intermediate is used to denote its positioning between the primary syllabus with VT-10 and the advanced syllabus with VT-86. The intermediate syllabus has stages in advanced navigation and strike (advanced formation flying).

Throughout the intermediate syllabus, the student runs each event, planning the routes, talking to the controllers, and getting the aircraft to the target.

Strike involves more advanced formation flying, for example, flying low-level with a wing man and learning how to work together as a section. The syllabus prepares the student for the advanced syllabus with the VT-86 flown in the much faster T-45C Goshawk.

Discussing the squadron's instructor cadre, Cdr Agostinelli said: "All instructors with VT-10 are pilots, a deliberate choice to help with reinforcing the basics of flying, with the focus of being a good crew member. Can you run a checklist? Can you handle an emergency procedure? Can you think clearly while other things are going on?

"Students fly in the front cockpit during the familiarisation stage because they're flying (though not for take-off or landing) and for most of the remainder of the syllabus, they're in the aft cockpit. When in the front cockpit, the instructor can observe what the student is doing to some extent by watching for student inputs on his displays and can observe where their hands are, when they're writing down and when they're doing things by using the small mirrors on the canopy rail. Ultimately, it's really about the communication between the two of us."

Every student has a class advisor who goes through their training with them. Their advisor is also their point of contact, if other things come up throughout the syllabus, so if other instructors note them struggling in certain areas, the advisor is the point of contact for the other instructors.

Student grading is conducted throughout the syllabus. The student must meet the minimum standard required for each stage to move to the next stage. The familiarisation, navigation and operational navigation stages have a check ride at the end of the stage. If the student fails to complete a stage, they get another opportunity to successfully complete that stage in accordance with CNATRA's training policies. "We don't try to weed out any of the students. We want them to succeed at VT-10 and move on to that spot in the fleet," said Cdr Agostinelli.

Once a student completes their course at VT-10 they move to VT-86 for advanced NFO training.

Sabrehawks

Anyone that arrives at VT-86 has already been selected for the F/A-18 Super Hornet

Above: **Training Squadron 10 (VT-10) 'Wild Ducks' uses weather shelters at Naval Air Station Pensacola, each shelter houses two T-6A Texan II aircraft.**
Mark Ayton

or the EA-18G Growler to complete the advanced NFO training programme following a syllabus which lasts between 31 and 37 weeks.

Commander George Zintak, commanding officer VT-86 said: "Our goal is to get the students through the syllabus and to the fleet replacement squadron [FRS] to learn how to operate a tactical aircraft, and then to the fleet to assume

the role of electronic warfare officer in the EA-18G Growler or weapon systems officer in the F/A-18 Super Hornet.

"VT-86's role is to refine the skills that the students have learned at VT-10 and expose them to the types of events they can expect to see out in the fleet: basic NFO checklists, all weather intercepts, close air support, and basic fighter manoeuvres. Once they complete the

Right: **T-6A Texan II BuNo 166000/ F000 stands tethered to the ramp at Naval Air Station Pensacola, Florida.**
Mark Ayton

of simulators before they fly the jet. They must pass all their familiarisation sims on the cockpit and the layout, then they use trainers to make sure they're able to handle emergency procedures and are familiar with the aircraft's systems and the systems knowledge required. Then they start the flying stages of the course.

Explaining the course sequence, Cdr Zintak said: "The syllabus starts with the familiarisation stage designed to learn the T-45 systems and the emergency procedures. Then they go through sims initially to get comfortable in the jet with the system set-up and practice emergency situations. Once complete, they fly instrument flights, to learn how the jet flies by flying around, shooting different approaches and to practice some of the capabilities of the jet.

"The next phase is strike where they learn how to incorporate some of the tactical stuff with their basic knowledge. This is very task saturated work for a student. They're calculating timing to hit a time on target. Strike also introduces them to section procedures, flying with a wingman for the first time and moving the aircraft dynamically.

"Following strike, they typically go to close air support or CAS which is probably the phase that most closely resembles the tactics used in the fleet. They're given a scenario and introduced to division flight ops, so up to four jets with them in the lead. They work with troops in a simulated scenario to practice attacks on targets and support friendlies on the ground.

"After CAS they get a BFM mission, which is one-on-one air combat in close-proximity and is designed to provide the student an opportunity to get visual sight pictures while flying in air-to-air combat."

The final phase is dedicated to all weather intercepts, where the student starts to learn about the mechanics of air-to-air engagements. Everything from intercepting aircraft to employing missiles on multiple groups of adversaries, while following a generic timeline to make sure they're executing the tactics correctly.

Cdr Zintak said: "We hold an annual NFO symposium where the students get to see the aircraft they're about to fly at the FRS. But more importantly, the fleet squadron training officers and the operations officers usually attend to discuss what it is we're doing well, what it is we're doing poorly, what they need more of, and what they want to see more of.

"That was how the CAS stage was developed. Initially, CAS was not taught at VT-86, but the FRS requested that we give students exposure to the CAS mission to reduce the amount of time spent by FRS instructors explaining what they're doing. Same thing with carrier operations [CV ops]. The FRS requested that we undertake more practice because the students were not good at the procedures. So, we've added more CV ops into our syllabus, and we've added in a simulator so they can practice their CV procedures. Anytime we make a big change it must be run through CNATRA.

"We've already seen the rewards of incorporating the CV op sim and have received good reviews specifically from the Super Hornet fleet replacement squadrons. FRS students are that little bit better, so the events they are scheduled for will go better and they won't require re-flying missions or adding more events

prescribed course, VT-86 instructors determine if the student has reached the threshold where they're good enough to go to the FRS, then we give them our blessing and they go to the FRS."

To mitigate the risk associated with transitioning a student from a T-6 into a T-45, VT-86 puts them through a series

Below: **VT-86 operates T-45C BuNo 163650/ F600 in stylised markings as the Training Air Wing 6 CAG-bird.**
Mark Ayton

because the students are not meeting the bar on that metric.

"We're also trying to incorporate a flight leadership phase, one that's just section work, section emergency, section procedures, which helps the transition between the fam stage and the strike stage, because in the strike stage, they're learning how to operate as a section, as well as doing the strike syllabus, which consists of low-levels, and weapons employments.

"CNATRA asked us to introduce the flight leadership phase to help with the burden of the transition by allowing students to just focus on section procedures before they're evaluated on those procedures. The flight leadership phase has been proposed to CNATRA. If approved, the proposed flight leadership phase will follow the initial fam sims and fam flights and will involve flying basic sections, basic section manoeuvring, and divisions. Then they'll receive a tactical mission ahead of the strike phase of the syllabus, and that's more in line with what the FRS does."

Student Grading

Discussing the grading guide and methods used by VT-86 instructors, Cdr Zintak said: "We have a guide called the master curriculum guide (MCG), which delineates the standard set for the student. As an instructor, we're supposed to be impartial, and we grade according to the MCG. So, in a strike event, for example, they could be executing a low-level route to a pre-planned time-on-target, or high-level for a medium altitude strike with a pre-planned time-on-target.

"So, for the strike event, the instructor is making sure they're able to handle the internal checklists and getting the aircraft ready to fight. During the mission portion, we're looking for turn point procedures where we want to make sure they're analysing fuel and time in addition to the position on the route.

"Essentially, we're getting them out of the admin phase they learned at VT-10, where they learned how to navigate and now trying to incorporate that into a tactical environment. It's very basic, but we have a set standard that we grade them to. Gradings awarded are a pass, an unset or incomplete due to a certain scenario that happened. Within that are individual graded items that we're looking at during a certain evolution. That is all based off a certain standard, we call them manoeuvre item files (MIFs), which refer to see where the student is expected to be at that point in training.

"The debrief is where most of the learning occurs. You can correct a student; they may fix the problem, but a lot of the learning comes from talking about what happened, how it went wrong, how to

Above: **T-45C BuNo 167098/ F622 taxies from its shelter for an early evening flight at Naval Air Station Pensacola.** Mark Ayton

Below: **A section of Goshawks await clearance to taxi for an early evening flight at Pensacola. The aircraft had to wait for the storm seen in the background of this shot to pass through the area.** Mark Ayton

recognise it, and how to correct it. That's how we improve the next event.

"There's an event at the end of each stage which is typically graded to a slightly higher standard than the student needs to reach because we want to make sure they've learned from the previous debrief points, and they're meeting the training standards by the end of that event.

"As they get to the end of the course, overall grading is an end average of how they did throughout the entire syllabus. That is sent to the folks that make the decision on whether a student gets Growler or Super Hornet. However, if a student does not perform to standard, then that's when we will get involved and meet with them one on one, see if there's any personal factors going on. Anything that we need to know about that could be detracting their performance. And then at that point, if other people need to get involved, that's when we coordinate all the procedures required."